People, Self-Coaching and Management Skills

An environmentally friendly book printed and bound in England by www.printondemand-worldwide.com

Mixed Sources
Product group from well-managed forests, and other controlled sources
www.fsc.org Cert no. TT-COC-002641
© 1996 Forest Stewardship Council

PEFC Certified
This product is from sustainably managed forests and controlled sources
www.pefc.org

PEFC/16-33-415

This book is made entirely of chain-of-custody materials

FastPrint
Publishing
www.fast-print.net/store.php

People, Self-Coaching and Management Skills
Copyright © Russ Baleson 2013

ISBN: 978-178035-665-5

First published 2013 by
FASTPRINT PUBLISHING
Peterborough, England.

Contents

Foreword

The toughest job in the world is not sales. It's not marketing. No, not product development. Or even new business. No, the toughest job is people. Most often the people in your own organisation. And that's because dealing with them begins with dealing with yourself. It's quite remarkable to come across an individual who is unafraid to tell you that. Especially someone who relies on staying in your good graces in order to stay in business. But Russ Baleson's irrepressible passion, drive and wealth of experience dealing with all levels of personnel and all manner of behaviours give him the confidence to speak truth to power. Gently. Convincingly. Persuasively. And effectively.

This collection of insights, observations, skills and tools, culled from his three decades of work as a respected trainer and coach, is an invaluable compendium of assets for managers and personnel alike. Dip into them at your leisure or reach for them in a crisis. Either way, when you find yourself or your organization in need of guidance dealing with the world's toughest job, reach out to Russ. Then engage, experience, learn and grow. Not just your business ... but yourself.

Lannon Tanchum

Lannon Tanchum is an award-wining Creative Director, marketing strategist and Agency Executive on accounts such as Porsche, Mercedes-Benz, Xerox, DHL, South African Breweries, Castrol, Amex, Toyota, Nissan, KLM, General Electric, Leading Hotels of the World and Halston amongst others.

Introduction

Russ Baleson is a training expert with over thirty years of professional experience. He is best known as a highly effective trainer and coach and has designed and facilitated numerous skill-building and life-changing workshops in both the United Kingdom and South Africa. His key distinguishable strength is the passion and skill he brings to impact and affect a positive behaviour change in each individual, coupled with his courage to challenge outdated training paradigms.

These tips and techniques were originally intended to support and reinforce some of the key concepts of his training programmes. However, it soon became clear that they could be used and enjoyed as a stand-alone reference. This is a collection of twenty-five of some of Russ's most popular articles and self-coaching checklists.

Originally from Johannesburg, South Africa, Russ now runs Russ Baleson Training in the United Kingdom.

Gravitas
Calm; Professional; Respectful; Dignified; Your Intention Heard and Felt

What is Gravitas?

Do you know someone who has natural gravitas? Think of those people who command respect by the way they present themselves. Gravitas is a learned or acquired capability - a calm, steady, measured approach that earns attention and respect from others.

I remember some of my school teachers. There were those emotional, almost panicky individuals who constantly battled to control the class. Then there were those who caned us for the slightest transgression and so we behaved, but only out of fear and we didn't necessarily learn much. But then there were those individuals who addressed us as adults in a confident, calm and steady manner. They maintained eye-contact, and earned our respect and attention.

And what about the parent who has something serious to address? It's natural to respond emotionally after having repeated the same messages day after day. But when parents purposely and calmly address a child's specific behaviour, they have an immediate impact.

Practical tips to help you project gravitas

Ensure that your emotions are under control

It's not always practical to wait until you are completely calm before addressing some issues but it is important that you behave calmly when doing so.

Speak at a calm and measured pace

Practise speaking with gravitas (yes, it takes practice). At first it can feel strange speaking so slowly and deliberately but it won't appear strange to others.

Talk softly

It is not necessary to raise your voice to be heard. Speaking loudly or shouting often provokes a defend/attack response.

Use silence and pauses

- Become comfortable with silence before speaking, after you've made a point, and when you have said enough.
- Make an impact even before you open your mouth by considering what you are about to say before you say it. Start with a few seconds of eye-contact and then once you've made the connection, begin to speak calmly.

- Pause for a few seconds to allow significant points to sink in. Ensure you maintain eye-contact whilst doing so.
- When you have made your point, stop talking.
- When someone else is speaking, give them your undivided attention and try to understand what they are saying. Listening to understand will create a reciprocal gravitas.
- When they have finished speaking, don't rush to answer. Wait a few seconds and consider what they have said before responding.
- If someone interrupts you, let them. It is pointless trying to talk when someone else is talking and they are certainly not listening at that time. Wait until they are finished before speaking.

Maintain a relaxed and confident posture

Leaning forward might be perceived as aggressive, and slouching could be perceived as submissive. Relax and maintain a confident posture.

Face the person you are addressing

It is important to face the person you are addressing. Be on the same level (avoid physically talking down to people), and maintain eye-contact.

Speak consciously

Keep it simple and to the point. It's more about the quality than the quantity.

Eliminate 'Irritators'

Irritators are unconscious words or phrases that have the potential to irritate others. These words or phrases don't add anything to the communication and very often create a barrier. Many people find themselves unconsciously using Irritators as 'fillers' because they are not comfortable with silence. This often undermines their intended communication. For example, as soon as someone says, "*With the greatest respect...*" you can be sure that an insult is about to follow.

Irritators are normal, everyone uses them. Most people won't notice when you use them. But when you consciously eliminate them from your language, you immediately improve the impact of your message, the clarity of your intention, and your Gravitas.

Be aware of the following and any other unconscious words or phrases when you are communicating. Listen to others, ask for feedback, record yourself, and watch how, by eliminating these words and phrases you can have an immediate positive impact.
- *With respect.*
- *Don't take this the wrong way / I don't want to be funny, but....*
- *Obviously* (for example - "Obviously you'd agree).
- *At the end of the day* (it gets dark?).
- *But...* (as in, "You really approached the project in a positive manner, but...).
- *I understand how you feel.*
- *It goes without saying.*
- *It's not rocket science.*
- *Let me level with you / To be honest / To be perfectly frank.*
- *You know /You know what I mean.*
- *You must understand that...*
- Plus any unnecessary jargon, swearing etc.

Eliminate unnecessary 'Softeners'

Good communication is clear, concise and to the point. 'Softeners' can reduce the impact of your entire message. Look out for any of these unnecessary words and phrases when you are speaking. For example, *"I'm sorry to bother you but, I think that it would possibly be a little bit better, if you could perhaps, you know, if it's not too much trouble, send it to me directly, if that's okay with you?"* Leaving out the unnecessary softeners would communicate your message clearly and assertively, *"Could you please send it to me directly so that I can work on it right away."* Typical softeners include:

- *I think* (when you are sure).
- *Sort of.*
- *Kind of.*
- *Perhaps.*
- *Possibly.*

There are situations when it is important to soften your message in order to be sensitive. However, there are many times when it is inappropriate and undermines your assertiveness and credibility. When you project yourself positively and with gravitas, people will respond accordingly.

Use it to show appreciation

Gravitas is also a wonderful technique to use when addressing positive behaviour. The gravitas communicates the sincerity of your praise. Positive feedback is specific information about what someone is doing well. It is important always to let them know exactly what you think was done well and why you like it. This will ensure that the feedback is seen to be sincere and the specific behaviour is repeated.

Inspire With Confidence

People with higher levels of gravitas tend to be noticed, listened to, respected, and followed. Gravitas is closely related to assertiveness and charisma, it conveys confidence and authenticity. It enables us to influence and inspire others. It is useful for leading others, coaching, training, selling, presenting, negotiating, and developing all kinds of relationships.

Professional Detachment for Managers
Maintaining Credibility

Managers will often be called upon to deal with issues that could have emotive connotations. The decisions they make could have far-reaching implications, either for their personal well-being or for that of their colleagues and subordinates. They could also lead to heated debate and argument. In such situations, managers cannot afford to let their own personal feelings or motives cloud the issues. Nor can they allow other people to pressure them into particular decisions for emotional reasons, or on the grounds of self-interest. Instead, they must be capable of making a professional decision and it must be made with reference to the best interests of the business as a whole. A person with professional detachment will appreciate the importance of this approach and will have no hesitation in making unpopular decisions if necessary.

A manager represents the company and acts as a role-model at all times. If, for example, managers socialise with employees after hours and behave in a way inappropriate to their role, they are putting themselves in a compromising position. They will find it difficult to maintain the respect of others thereafter. And so they will find it more difficult to influence others' behaviour.

Your tolerance determines the level of your professionalism as well as the stability of your mood and mental state when faced with difficult situations. Professional detachment means mastering techniques that help you distance yourself from emotions during these awkward and difficult situations. It is about adopting a new attitude towards what is happening regardless of its intensity. It helps you to look at events objectively without reacting impulsively or emotionally or taking what happens as a personal matter. Setting yourself apart from the events and observing them dispassionately prevents any display of uncontrolled emotions.

Since what you feel appears in your face, voice and body movements, it is important to prepare yourself before getting involved in what it may become a difficult interaction or a controversial issue. When you are emotionally involved in a difficult situation, your voice is affected, your body can begin to shake, and even the colour of your face can change. Nobody wants to be out of control. This is where being aware of, and practising professional detachment will help you deal with these situations in a calm and responsible manner.

The best strategy for remaining calm and cool in tough times is to develop sufficient resources and qualities to increase your tolerance levels. This is not something that can be mastered quickly. It requires the practice and evaluation of specific interpersonal skills. Remaining calm and responsible in emotive situations will not only help you to deal with any type of situation objectively, it will also gain you respect and admiration.

Essential Features of the Professionally Detached Manager

- Stands back from issues; does not become emotionally or personally involved.

- Is even-tempered; is not prone to mood swings or outbursts of temper.

- Does not get involved in petty arguments.

- Identifies with management.

- Can detach from own and others' personal interests to make professional, optimal decisions.

- Will present a consistent and calm image to others.

- When involved in discussion or argument conducts himself/herself with dignity and decorum.

- Does not make personal comments or take things personally.

- When faced with conflict, will disregard personal interest (his/her own or the group's), in favour of professionally optimal choices.

- Will make decisions and stick to them; is prepared to stand alone if challenged. Does not become defensive.

Quick Tips from Experienced Managers

Many experienced managers have gained their wisdom through hard work and self-evaluation. They have typically experienced frustration along the way using approaches that appeared to make good sense at the time. With experience, it is easy to see the mistakes that could be avoided. Here are a few common management mistakes it would be wise to avoid:

Training someone to do something they can already do

Think about it. How much of your time is spent teaching people something they already know? If a problem is not caused by a lack of skill - in other words, if the person could do it if they really wanted to - then training the person in order to fix the problem is a waste of time.

Most of the time it's likely that the problem won't be caused by a genuine lack of skill. People will usually be able to do what's expected of them except, of course, people who are new to their jobs or are doing a task that is new to them. Ask yourself, *"Could he or she do it if they really wanted to (or if their lives depended on it)?"* Training is an invaluable activity when it is focused on building skills and knowledge that is really needed.

Treating everyone exactly the same

There is nothing as unequal as the equal treatment of unequals. We are all individuals and deserve to be treated as such. Of course we should be held accountable to the same standards, but applying a blanket-management approach is a quick way to lose trust, credibility and motivation. The skilled manager will always change style and approach depending upon the individual they are dealing with, the current task under discussion, and the specific circumstances.

g the need to maintain credibility by always providing the answers to questions

An important role of any manager is to build the awareness, responsibility and self-esteem of their people. Always telling people what to do withholds responsibility and denies awareness. Involving and engaging individuals by expanding their thinking and letting them take the initiative to provide ideas and solutions, will not only enhance their self-esteem but also ensure their commitment and buy-in. You aren't helping by always telling them what to do, when to do it, and how to do it.

Treating others as you would like to be treated instead of treating others as THEY would like to be treated

The real intention of, 'Do unto others', is to consider how *they* want to be treated. What is their learning style? How do they prefer to take in information? It is most likely that they have different preferences to you and most of the time this can be accommodated.

Avoiding confrontation and difficult conversations

The quicker an issue or behaviour is addressed, the easier it is to have the conversation. Not having the conversation can be perceived as condoning the behaviour. These discussions require certain skills. It is easy to deliver a difficult message and leave the person feeling de-motivated, but it takes skill, gravitas, and diplomacy to deliver it whilst maintaining self-esteem and motivation. Best to get skilled up fast! The problem won't go away by ignoring it.

Assuming that your values are common-sense and expecting the same from others

We tend to judge people when they don't behave the way we would behave. You hear someone say, "*He has no manners!*" It is most likely that he does have manners; they are just different to the way you would do things.

Assuming that everyone's big motivator is money

Of course money is very important to most people but it is what the money represents to that person, at that particular time, that is the true motivator. Is it to provide an education for their children? To fund a holiday in the Bahamas? To have their teeth whitened? Make a point of knowing as much as possible about your people, their values, their preferences, their goals, and their dreams.

Assuming that the only consequences that affect behaviour, are disciplinary in nature

Too many managers use the threat of disciplinary procedures to motivate their team. And even more often, managers fail to focus on providing *positive* consequences. A consequence is *an act or instance of following something as an effect, result, or outcome*. Feedback is a consequence and so are promotion, praise, and attention. Whether it be positive or negative, a consequence can only be effective if it is felt by the person you are directing it to. *So make it matter to them*. Once again, we are all different and moved or motivated in different ways.

Assuming that what motivates you will also motivate others

Take the word, 'motivation' and place an 'e' after the 'v' and a 'c' after the 'a'. This gives you two words, 'motive' and 'action'. *Motivation means a Motive for Action.* We all have different motives. Some people are motivated by fame or recognition, some by security, some by being in control, etc. What motivates one person may have no significant appeal for others. It is very important to know your people well in order to influence them or to *move* them to action.

Assuming expectations are crystal clear

Most of the time we assume that expectations are crystal clear because it seems to be common sense. Frank Zappa said, *"There is no such thing as common sense, good sense is rare!"* Just because it is crystal clear to you doesn't mean it is to anyone else. The easiest way to check if your expectations are clear is to ask, *"If someone else asked that person what I expected them to do in a certain situation, what would they say? What would their actual words be?"*

Trying to be liked instead of gaining respect

Most managers befriend their people and try hard to be liked. People will like you when they respect you, when they are getting value out of your relationship, not just enjoyment.

Focusing mostly on tasks or mostly on people, instead of maintaining a balance

It's important to keep the balance. Too often managers focus mostly on one particular part of the job. For example, if the focus is just on the task, then the people probably won't feel valued and will typically do just enough to stay out of trouble. An equal focus needs to be placed on the task, the individual, and the team.

Providing Feedback
Behaviour That's Rewarded Will Be Repeated!

Four-year-old Arthur has just spent three hours on his own in his bedroom teaching himself how to tie his shoelaces. He finally comes running out and says, *"Daddy, daddy, look! I can tie my own shoelaces!"* And his father says, *"Tuck your shirt in Arthur!"*

Managers and people in general have a natural inclination to look for the things that are wrong. Managers in particular are natural trouble-shooters and always on the lookout for problems, difficulties, faults, dangers, etc. Most managers don't naturally look for what is right. They may also find it a bit embarrassing to provide positive personal feedback.

Providing effective positive feedback is the easiest and most motivating way to shape someone's behaviour.

If you are a manager and feel a bit hesitant about telling people what you like about them or what you like about what they are doing, then get over it! This is an essential part of your role and once applied will not only motivate others, it will make you feel good too.

Most people understand the concept of *'Behaviour that is rewarded will be repeated'*. That is how we train animals and we have a natural tendency to 'train' children in the same way. Think about what a parent does the first time a child uses a potty. Why does the parent clap excitedly, laying on the praise as if it's the *best* thing he/she has ever seen? Part of the reason is it that they are proud but it's much more likely that they are relieved that the nappy phase is almost over. They realise that this will make their lives a lot easier and that positive feedback will ensure that this specific behaviour is repeated.

It is important however that feedback is communicated correctly so that the receiver knows that it is 100% sincere and *behaviourally* specific. Telling a child that he's been a good boy and expecting him to know the specific behaviour to repeat, is pointless. The same is true for adults. Praising a salesperson by saying, *"Well done! That was a brilliant sale"*, provides no substance for the person to judge the sincerity of the message and certainly no indication of the behaviour required to repeat the success.

How to Provide Feedback Effectively

All coaching, training, leadership, and management of people requires the use of effective feedback skills. This feedback, to be constructive and effective, needs to be communicated in such a way that the person feels motivated either to repeat successful behaviours, or improve on an unsatisfactory performance.

Positive Feedback

Positive feedback is specific information about what someone is doing well. To ensure your intention is communicated accurately, it is important *always* to provide a **'WHAT'** and a **'WHY'** in your feedback. In other words, the person must know exactly **what** was done well (the specific behaviour) and **why** you liked it. This will ensure that the feedback is seen to be sincere and that the specific behaviour is repeated. For example, *"I really admired the way you kept calm with that customer. He was quite aggressive and yet you let him finish, acknowledged his disappointment and calmly offered to fix the situation for him. I am so impressed with the way you manage your emotions."*

Feedback for Improvement

Feedback for improvement is specific information, about **WHAT** was done and **WHY** it wasn't effective. It is then followed up with **WHAT** the alternative is and **WHY** it would have been more effective. It is preferable where appropriate, to pull the second 'what and why' from the other person.

For example, *"I noticed that when the customer said they didn't understand, you repeated what you had just said and the customer was no clearer. It would have been better if you had asked the customer at that stage what they weren't clear about so that you could explain that particular point in a different way."*

Or even better, to involve the person in a coaching style: *"I noticed that when the customer said they didn't understand, you repeated what you had just said and the customer was no clearer. What could you have done at that stage that would have helped you to get through to that customer?* Once they have answered, ask, *"And how would that have helped?"* This gets them to provide the second 'what and why'.

Maintaining Self-Esteem

The 'what' ensures that the focus is on a specific behaviour rather than on a person's character. Consider the difference between, *"What's wrong with you, you're so unreliable?"* and, *"You said you would bring me the report by five and you didn't, so I didn't have the stats I needed for the meeting"*.

Summary Guidelines

There are several guidelines to follow when giving effective feedback:

- Don't pay compliments just to make someone feel good. Your intention needs to be honest and sincere. Don't say that something was done well when it wasn't and if you can't think of anything good to say, then stay quiet.
- Feedback must be delivered with gravitas, calmly at a measured pace, directly, with eye-contact and letting the person hear and feel your sincerity.
- We often give feedback based on results; this doesn't have the same impact as *behavioural* feedback. Don't respond too quickly with feedback until you know exactly what the person has done (rather than just achieved). Ask questions and listen carefully to *how* they have achieved it, and then you can reinforce the specific behaviour.

- **Don't ever use the word, *'but'* or *'however'*** when giving feedback. It's annoying, disrespectful and manipulative. Trying to hide uncomfortable feedback in-between positive feedback makes the good feedback appear insincere. So many managers have been taught the 'Pat-Kick-Pat' approach to providing feedback or perhaps you know it as the 'Sandwich Technique'. This is the technique of starting with positive feedback, sneaking in the negative feedback, and then quickly ending with more positive feedback. Keep it separate. If your intention is to give positive feedback, give it anywhere and in front of anyone. If you want to give feedback for improvement, give it privately, in a calm environment, focusing on the specific behaviour rather than the person's character.
- Don't give vague or unsupported feedback. *Always* supply the reason.   Be specific about what was said or done and why you feel the behaviour was effective.
- When offering Feedback for Improvement, tell, or ask the person what could have been said or done that would have been better and why it would have been better.
    - WHAT was done and WHY it wasn't effective.
    - WHAT could have been done and WHY that would have been better.
- *Always* maintain the person's self-esteem.
- Don't focus only on very good or very bad behaviour. Examine the average performance as well and provide feedback for effort, improvement, etc. Providing behavioural feedback when someone is making an effort will help them achieve the goal much faster than without it.

Try this at home!

These interpersonal skills are effective with anyone, in any situation, and will have a significant positive impact on all your relationships.

Where to begin?

Why not start immediately by taking a tip from author, Stephen Levine:

> **"If you had an hour to live and could only make one phone call,**
> **Who would you call?**
>
> **What would you say?**
>
> **And why are you waiting?"**

Listening Skills
There are those who listen and there are those who wait to talk!

Even though listening skills can be learned, *not everyone can improve their listening skills by learning them*. People learn best and most easily when the skills they are learning are consistent with their beliefs, values and motives. **You can't be a good listener if you're not interested** in what someone is saying. You will develop your skills much faster by learning how to become deeply interested in another person. For those who *are* interested in other people and want to improve their ability to listen, read on.

Dr Steven Covey ('*The Seven Habits of Highly Effective People*') describes five levels of listening:

Level 1. Not Listening
This is self-explanatory.

Level 2. Pretending to Listen
How many times have you been guilty of pretending to listen? At some level we all sense if someone is not really engaged with what we are saying no matter how much nodding of the head or affirmative sounds they are making.

Level 3. Selective Listening
Paul Simon wrote the famous song, 'The Boxer' in 1968 and in it expresses this level of listening very clearly, "Still a man hears what he wants to hear and disregards the rest".

Level 4. Attentive Listening
Attentive listening has been described as paying attention and focusing energy on the words that are being said. Most people have attended some kind of business training where the following list of techniques have been taught to improve listening skills:
- Facing the person and maintaining eye-contact.
- Leaning slightly forward.
- Maintaining open body-language, open palm gestures, unfolded arms.
- Making appropriate facial gestures.
- Making acknowledging noises such as '*yes*', '*I see*', '*okay*', '*uh-huh*', '*right*', etc.
- Having a good posture.
- Nodding the head.

It might surprise you to learn that these techniques are often the cause of bad listening skills. The list is usually derived from observing good listeners who certainly display these behaviours. The problem is that whilst you are focusing on what your hands are doing or remembering to nod and make appropriate noises when the other person is speaking, your attention is on yourself, not on what the other person is saying. It's really all about the INTENTION, the mental process that drives those good listeners to behave the way they do. And that takes us to the most effective level of listening, level five, where your intention is to try and understand what the other person is saying.

Level 5. Listening To Understand

Most people listen from their own perspective, in other words, 'How does this affect me?' We need to strive to understand the other person's point of view, to listen from *their* perspective, not ours. How is what they are saying affecting *them*? How are *they* feeling about what they are saying?

If your intention is focused on their perspective and you are trying to understand what they are saying, you will really be listening. If you are listening to understand, your body language will be *naturally appropriate*. In other words, you will be facing the person, maintaining eye-contact, making appropriate sounds, and all of this will be perceived as genuine by the talker - because it is.

Reflecting Back

Another benefit of Listening to Understand is that it gives you the substance to feedback on what you sense and observe, such as their feelings, emotions, energy levels, etc. *"I noticed that you seemed a bit despondent when you spoke about that customer"*. This creates much more engagement and rapport and shows the person that you are truly listening to them.

It's Not Always Easy to be in the Room

Our minds are continually active and to focus attention solely on what someone else is saying is not always that easy. It takes a deliberate mental decision. Nigel Risner, in his book, 'The Impact Code', says, *"If you're in the room, be in the room"*. He is not only referring to the physical aspect of being in the room, but also about being *consciously and mentally* in the room, focusing on that moment and blocking out everything else.

What Makes It Difficult For You To Listen?

There are many things that make listening in today's fast, active world a challenging task. Be honest and ask yourself what makes it difficult for you to listen and you'll probably come up with the following reasons and perhaps many more:

- Not enough time.
- A lack of interest in the message.
- A negative reaction to the speaker.
- Being preoccupied with other matters.
- Not respecting what they have to say.
- Mentally judging or arguing with points made by the speaker before he or she has finished talking.
- Becoming bored with listening and preferring active involvement by talking.
- The poor delivery of the message - the tone, passion, articulation, enthusiasm, eye-contact, etc.

What Could You Do That Would Make It Easier For You To Listen?

Compare the way you listen to the suggestions in the following list:

- Face the person who is talking and maintain a comfortable level of eye-contact.
- Maintain a comfortable distance that is appropriate for both of you.
- Give your undivided attention and refrain from doing anything else at that time. *"You cannot truly listen to anyone and do anything else at the same time."* **M. Scott Peck**
- Get rid of any possible interruptions.
- Concentrate on what they are saying. See it from their point of view and try to understand what they are saying. Suspend your judgement and try to grasp the *meaning* of what they are saying.
- Stop any mental rehearsing you might be doing. Don't think of your next question or how you might reply. Try to understand what is being said at that moment.
- Wait three seconds after the person has finished talking before you say anything.

Application

Learning is not complete without application, without putting into practice what you have learned.

Set yourself a goal to listen to understand and rate yourself out of ten after each conversation. Just the act of trying to understand will improve your listening skills and therefore have a significant positive impact on the quality of all your relationships.

"I know that you believe you understand what you think I said, but I'm not sure you realise that what you heard is not what I meant." *Robert McCloskey*

"The most basic of all human needs is the need to understand and be understood. The best way to understand people is to listen to them." *Ralph Nichols*

"Courage is what it takes to stand up and speak; courage is also what it takes to sit down and listen."
Winston Churchill

Challenging the Open Question Paradigm

A paradigm is a theory or belief system that guides the way we do things. It can be defined as a pattern or model; a set of assumptions, concepts, values, and practices that constitute a way of viewing reality. It's easy to buy into a paradigm when it makes sense and you know no better. It isn't however always the wisest thing to do.

This article challenges the paradigm of how to ask Open Questions. Millions of people have been taught that Open Questions start with the words 'Who' 'What' 'When' 'Where' 'Why' and 'How'. Do they really? Another paradigm many have bought into is that a Closed Question is one that provokes a 'yes' or 'no' answer and therefore, if someone can't reply with a *yes* or a *no*, then the question is Open. This is false logic.

The type of question does not depend upon how it is answered but rather on how well the intention has been communicated. You cannot control another's response. Sometimes a Closed Question will elicit a detailed response and vice-versa. By understanding the purpose of an Open Question however, you can give yourself the best chance of communicating your intention, being clearly understood, and receiving the type of response you are seeking.

Origin

The *'Five Ws and an H'* are questions that are effective in information-gathering. They are often mentioned in journalism, research, investigations, etc., about how to get the complete story on a subject. For example:

- *Who* is it about?
- *What* happened?
- *When* did it take place?
- *Where* did it take place?
- *Why* did it happen?
- *How* did it happen

This style of questioning usually uncovers the facts necessary for a report to be considered complete. But let's not confuse this with the concept of Open Questions.

Intention

What is the intention of an Open Question? It is to draw out a more detailed response; to encourage someone to open up (we should refer to them as Open-Up Questions). But let's speak plainly - **The purpose of an Open Question is to get the other person to talk lots**. Having clarity of purpose or intention, it's easy to test the paradigm. Take a look at the following:

- *Who* did you meet last night?
- *What* is your name?
- *When* did you get here?
- *Where* do you live?
- *Why* do you need to see him?
- *How* was school?

Do any of the above questions clearly communicate the real intention of an Open Question? In other words, **do any of them say, *without doubt*, 'Talk lots to me'?** If there is any doubt, then there is a chance that the intention won't be clearly understood. I'm sure that you are familiar with the question, *"How was school?"* How do children usually respond when asked this question? They certainly don't see it as an invitation to talk lots about their recent school activities. And what's more, this question is often asked when the child's attention is occupied in some activity or when the parent is multi-tasking, possibly packing away the groceries for example. And so overall, there is no way that the question can be perceived as a genuine request for lots of information. Consider the alternative of a parent waiting until the child is not involved in an activity, facing the child, maintaining a comfortable eye-contact and asking, *"Tell me more about some of the things you've been doing at school lately, I'd really like to know how things have been for you."* The chance of the child opening up is much better than just, *"How was school?"*

Another mistake that many make is trying to replace the *'who'*, *'what'*, *'when'*, etc., with other words or phrases. *Describe* to me in detail, *tell me*, *talk me through*, etc. are all phrases that appear to be an effective way of communicating the concept of 'Talk lots to me'. But if you are relying on a word or phrase to do the work for you then you may as well revert back to the old paradigm. If your intention is to get the person to open up to you, just think of the most obvious way you could communicate this in your own natural style. *"Describe to me absolutely everything you did this weekend"*, doesn't exactly sound like a genuinely interested and natural approach.

Questioning Comes From a Deep Interest

Our intentions towards others are determined by our beliefs and values and they run deep. They are not a collection of skills and techniques, and because humans have such excellent intent detectors, it has to be sincere. You are more likely to improve your questioning techniques by developing a genuine interest in others. Good questions come, just like active listening, from a deep interest and flow naturally from the dialogue.

Why Use Open Questions?

Good Open Questions can stimulate conversation, create comfortable rapport, allow freedom of expression (while you listen of course), and avoid the harsh interrogation style that using just Closed Questions creates.

Put It to the Test

Try it out now! Phrase a question in such a way that it is absolutely obvious that you want someone to talk lots, and notice the difference. And remember that as soon as someone begins to respond to your question, your role needs to change to that of *listener* if you really expect them to open up to you. You will find it a very effective and worthwhile paradigm shift.

Get That Job!
Give Yourself the Best Chance in an Interview

Most people are aware of the basic essentials for impressing a potential employer in an interview. These include presenting a professional C.V., dressing appropriately, being punctual, maintaining confident eye-contact, etc. Very few however, are aware of how to prepare in order to provide the interviewer with exactly what they are looking for.

These days, most Recruitment Agencies and Human Resource Consultants receive an overwhelming amount of online job applications so before we tell you how to put your best-self forward, let's remind you why you need to be conscientious with your application.

Assessment of a candidate does not start with the interview. For many jobs it is perfectly possible and indeed sometimes essential to eliminate the majority of applicants without interviewing them at all. This can be done through initial screening techniques and by examining the Application Form. The Application Form is much more valuable than is generally realised and provides a wealth of information about a candidate. Its main purpose is to elicit information to identify candidates whose skills and experience correspond closely to the job requirements. It is essential that you complete it in full. Employers will not excuse sloppiness! An applicant who does not care enough to complete the application form in detail is generally not a good bet to be conscientious on the job.

It is also important to ensure that the information on your C.V., your LinkedIn profile, and your Application Form is consistent and at the time of application reflects the job being applied for. Generic applications are convenient when you are actively job-seeking, but it is wise to take the time to tailor your experience and personal summary/bio to reflect the role you are applying for.

But let's get to the method that will give you the best chance of getting the job (if you are the most suitable candidate for that position).

The Interview - What Are They Looking For?

Interviewers are looking for information that will tell them about an applicant's qualifications and motivations for the job so that they can match that against the job criteria. During the interview they want to gain information about an applicant's aptitudes, education and experience to determine if he or she has the ABILITY to do the job. They also need to determine if the applicant WILL do the job once hired by taking a close look at the types of factors that have motivated past performance. Then by combining the applicant's ABILITY to do the job with the applicant's MOTIVATION to do it, the interviewer can more accurately predict future success. The interviewer constantly has three main objectives in mind when conducting an interview, and they are:

1. Is the person suitable?

The main purpose is to assess face-to-face impact and establish whether the candidate meets the selection criteria. Is the person suitable for the job? Is this the kind of job that they would really like to apply themselves to?

2. Do they have an accurate picture of the job?

The applicant should be given a full understanding of what the job entails. It is pointless to gloss over aspects that the interviewer thinks may be unattractive. If in fact they are unattractive to that candidate, it is far better that he or she should withdraw the application for the position rather than discover them later when already employed.

3. Non-discriminatory

Their third objective is to conduct the interview in a fair and non-discriminatory manner.

Past Behaviour Is the Most Reliable Indicator of Future Behaviour

Most recruitment professionals base their strategy on facts and evidence rather than theoretical supposition. The strategy that they use to gather this information will also help you to prepare for, and make a positive impression during the interview. And even if they don't use this strategy, if you use the following method, you will be able to will give them what they need to make an optimum decision.

Let's take a look at the **BAR** strategy, (**B**ackground, **A**ction, **R**esult) to enable you to provide adequate and relevant information so that your interviewer can match your knowledge, skills and experience to the job being considered.

Background

The Background provides the framework from within which an interviewer is able to assess the relevance and impact of your behaviour. For example consider the statement, "I managed a team which achieved all its targets". It doesn't tell you how big the team was or anything at all about the challenge or the targets. It doesn't explain the nature of the economy at the time or anything else to make the achievement significant. In other words, it is the Background that positions and provides perspective to what you have done.

Action

The Action describes specifically what you did in a given situation. Interviewees often talk about what '*they*' achieved, for example, "*We* designed a new quality process". That does not explain what *your* role was and what *you* actually did. The interviewer is looking for specific behaviours that will give an indication of how you will most probably behave in the future.

Result

The Result describes the outcome of your particular action. This is what they are looking for. They need to know what was achieved as a result of your specific action in those circumstances.

How to Prepare for That Interview

The best way to prepare for an interview is to consider the questions you know they could ask you. If you are interviewing for a sales position you know they will probably ask you questions about your sales ability, negotiation skills, sales results, customer service, product knowledge, ability to work under pressure, knowledge of the market-place, etc. So take each of these areas and prepare **BARs** for them. For example, under the heading of Customer Service, think back to a few occasions when you provided excellent Customer Service and list a few **BARs**. For example:

Background: A customer, who had been buying from us for a number of years, had four of his orders delivered late and as a result did not want to buy from us in the future.

Action: As soon as I heard about this, I went to see him and explained how sorry I was for the poor service that he had received. I explained that I would really like to understand his delivery requirements to see if I could find a way of meeting his needs. During the discussion I listened attentively and responded with empathy by saying things like, "That must have been frustrating," until he finally felt understood. When I asked him if he had any ideas as to how we could meet his needs in the future, he suggested that he could email his order at the beginning of each week. I agreed that I would check my emails each Monday morning and process his orders immediately. I gave him my private number as well for reassurance.

Result: Over the past year he has always received his orders on time and as a result has spent twice as much as he did the previous year. I have also gained two new clients as a result of his recommendations since then.

Once you have prepared numerous **BARs** for each of the potential areas that they are likely to ask, you need to learn them. And when the time for the interview arrives, you need to relax and weave the information into your natural style so that they get a sense of who you are, what you have done, how you have done it, what you have achieved, and how closely you fit the requirements for the job at hand. This method of preparation will also enable you to measure the job against your own preferences.

Caution!

Skilled interviewers have many methods to determine how truthful your answers are. They will ask questions in a number of ways to check consistency and will also follow-up with questions to understand the reasons and motivation behind your answers. You will look foolish and have no chance of getting the job if your answers have not been factual.

We spend most of our time at work and it affects our lives in many ways. It makes sense to invest the time and effort into ensuring that the interviewer sees you in the best possible light and that you gain enough information to determine whether the job will meet your personal needs and enable you to reach your potential.

Are SMART Objectives Really Smart?
How to Set Effective Behavioural Objectives

There are some training models that have stood the test of time and as such have secured a place in our library of jargon. Does this mean that they are sacred? It seems as if most people are not willing to question or challenge these concepts even if they don't seem effective at times.

Most business people have been taught the SMART method to set objectives and many find it rather cumbersome. This is because there is a tendency to get tied up in the theoretical process rather than clearly defining the intended end-result. I have worked with many Human Resources Consultants, Managers, and Trainers and almost every one of them has been taught, or has taught the concept of SMART Objectives. I have however come across very few who can quickly and easily set an effective objective.

What is an Objective?

An objective is an intent communicated by a statement of what the person will be doing when they have successfully completed the objective. In other words, it is a description of the *behaviour* we want the person to demonstrate. When the element of clearly defined behaviour is lacking in an objective, the expectations are confusing, and it's almost impossible to evaluate whether the objective has been successfully achieved.

A more simple and effective way of setting objectives is to focus on the concept of *observable behaviour*.

A **Behavioural Objective** has three components:

Behaviour	The *observable* behaviour.
Standards	How well the person must perform the behaviour.
Conditions	The conditions under which the person must be exhibiting the behaviour. The timing, frequency, restraints, circumstances, etc.

Each objective must contain a **Behaviour**, *and wherever appropriate, either or both* **Standards** and **Conditions**.

Behaviour - Is It Observable?

A meaningfully stated objective is one that succeeds in communicating your intent. There are however many words that are open to a wide range of interpretation. What do you really mean when you state in an objective that you want someone to *understand*, or *fully appreciate*, or *know how* to do something? It is very important to make your intention explicit by describing what the person will actually be doing when demonstrating that he or she *understands* or *appreciates*, etc. In other words, you need to describe 'What the behaviour looks like'. For example, instead of '*Update your digital knowledge*', it would be far more effective to say, '*Watch and summarise the contents of the Click programme on BBC1*'. But this in itself is still not an effective objective.

Standards - How Well?

Once you have described what it is you want the person to be able to do, you can increase the quality of an objective by telling the person *how well* you want them to be able to do it. If you can specify at least the minimum acceptable performance for each objective, you will have a standard against which to measure the results. One of the most obvious ways is to specify a **time limit** where one is appropriate. Other appropriate standards might include, **minimum number** (obtaining at least three examples from their team); **number of correct attempts** (getting at least seven correct out of the list of ten); **quality required** (calculations must be accurate to at least three significant figures), etc. For example, *'Watch and summarise in one-thousand words, the contents of the Click programme on BBC1, by the end of the week'*.

It is not always possible to specify a standard with as much detail as you would like, but this should not prevent you from trying to communicate, as fully as possible, the intention required.

Conditions

Simply stating the Behaviour and the Standards may not be enough to prevent misunderstanding. Are there any important procedures that must be followed? Will guidelines be provided? Under what circumstances must the behaviour be applied? The answer to each of these questions will make a difference in the interpretation of the objective. What will the person be allowed to use, be provided with, be denied, etc.? Consider the givens, restrictions, circumstances, and frequency that will enable you to describe the Conditions, for example, *'Given a list of...'* or *'In front of a prospective customer...'* or *'Referring to the policy guidelines...'*

Keep it Simple

To avoid getting side-tracked by the theory (as most do with SMART objectives), it is important to keep the process simple. Simply identify the observable behaviour and then add any Conditions and Standards that will make the Behaviour crystal clear and measurable. Sometimes, the distinction between Conditions and Standards may be unclear and this does not matter. As long as the objective clearly communicates **what the person will be doing** when they have successfully completed the objective, **how well they will be doing it**, and **under what conditions**, the objective will achieve its purpose.

For example, *'Compile fifty phone numbers of potential customers from the BestData list that don't appear on our records by the end of this week'*.

Measurement

Behavioural objectives make the concept of measurement quick and effective. Did the person produce a one-thousand word summary of the BBC1 Click programme by the end of the week? Or, did the person compile fifty phone numbers of potential customers from the BestData list that don't appear on their records by the end of the week? Yes? - objective achieved. No? - objective not achieved.

Is it Smart?

If you are still determined to hang on the SMART Paradigm, rest assured that a Behavioural Objective will always be SMART. Put it to the test. Try and set an objective the easy way and then measure it against the SMART model.

Goal Setting

Specific
Measurable
Achievable
Realistic
Timely

SPECIFIC - An observable Behaviour will always be specific.

MEASURABLE - An observable Behaviour with Standards and Conditions lists a detailed outcome and will therefore always be measurable.

AGREED / **A**CHIEVABLE - If it is observable, it will be achievable and unless objectives are discussed and agreement gained, there will be little commitment to achieve them. 'Agreed' in this context really refers to the process of communicating the objective and not to the way it is written.

REALISTIC - The Behaviour, Conditions and Standards, force you to assess the relevance and practicality of the objective and will automatically be realistic.

TIMELY / **T**IME RELATED - One of the Standards.

SMART is only one of many business tools and certainly not a one-size-fits-all method. Look for, and encourage, other effective techniques that fit your purpose.

A Paradigm Shift

In this dynamic age of fast-changing technology and challenging economic times, it is important to evaluate the familiar. It makes sense to check assumptions, models, and methods to find easier, quicker, and often more effective ways of achieving results.

Affirmations for a Happier Life

We all talk to ourselves, positively or negatively. In other words, you use affirmations whether you realise it or not. The affirmations you use are in the form of quotations, idioms, proverbs, sayings, and knowledge that you've gained throughout your life as well as quotes from people who you've allowed to influence and shape your thinking, either consciously or unconsciously.

You can however *choose* the affirmations you want to shape your life.

An affirmation is a positive, believable thought that you choose to embed in your consciousness to produce a desired result

Rather than wade through the theory behind affirmations, let's get right down to practicalities so that you can experience the impact and benefits first-hand.

Before you read further, here's a challenge for you. Don't just glance over the content. Read the following twenty affirmations OUT LOUD and WITH FEELING and take note of what resonates and how it makes you feel. In the spaces below replace the xxxxxxxxxxxs with your name as you read each one aloud.

- I xxxxxxxxxxxxxx project confidently and positively in all situations by using positive language, refraining from criticism and complaints, displaying a can-do attitude, and keeping my spirits high.

- I xxxxxxxxxxxxxx let go - I choose confrontations wisely.

- I xxxxxxxxxxxxxx take responsibility for my own happiness, *right now* and choose to concentrate on what I have instead of what I lack.

- I xxxxxxxxxxxxxx live in truth, openness and integrity. I live my life on purpose and remain true to my values.

- I xxxxxxxxxxxxxx live as much of my life as I can right now. I find my greatest pleasure in the present moment, so whatever I am doing, I do it as well as I can.

- I xxxxxxxxxxxxxx take responsibility for my life. I am courageous; I *act* and make things happen. I embrace life and I choose to be happy.

- This is a big day for me. Today is a wonderful day, everything works out for me. Today I'm successful, today I am happy, today I grow in love.

- I xxxxxxxxxxxxxx commit myself to noticing when I rush. I can't smell the roses if I am running past them. As soon as I notice myself rushing, I bring myself back to the present moment.

- I xxxxxxxxxxxxx find my happiness by living in the moment rather than demanding that situations, conditions, places, or people make me happy.

- My energy is abundant, exciting, liberating, and affects everyone and everything around me in a positive way.

- I xxxxxxxxxxxxx make optimum use of my senses and live in a state of awareness, experiencing fully, all the wonderful facets of life. I trust and act on my intuition.

- I xxxxxxxxxxxxx enjoy the positive energy of health by giving and allowing my body appropriate nutrition, exercise, stimulation, relaxation and peace of mind.

- I xxxxxxxxxxxxx nurture friends by allowing them the freedom to be themselves, whilst giving them empathy, love and support. I grow my relationships with effective, honest and open communication.

- I xxxxxxxxxxxxx become what I think about all day long. The more attention I put on something that is positive, the better I feel. When I find myself trapped in my analytical mind, I drop my thoughts, clear my mind, and relax. I accept thoughts for what they are. There is no need to turn them into more than they really are or to take them too seriously.

- I xxxxxxxxxxxxx distrust and dismiss my thoughts when I am low. I wait until my mood lifts which happens quickly when I don't focus on negative thoughts.

- I xxxxxxxxxxxxx am happy with what is, rather than obsessing with what could be better.

- I xxxxxxxxxxxxx strive to be fully with the person I am with.

- I xxxxxxxxxxxxx am gentle on myself. I treat myself with compassion, love, humour and acceptance, *and above all,* I am true to myself.

- I xxxxxxxxxxxxx am stronger than temptation. I assert my will, take control, and then relax and enjoy my life.

How was that for you? These affirmations were written by someone else and when you create your own, you'll be amazed at how much more powerful they are and the positive results that follow. The use of affirmations rests on the concept that thought is creative, that what you think about, consciously or unconsciously, creates your experience. Affirmations are clear, desirable, positive thoughts. You choose affirmations deliberately to replace unclear, unwanted, negative thoughts.

The subconscious mind can be impressed like a piece of clay. The repetitive use of an affirmation will simultaneously make its impression on your mind and erase the old thought pattern, producing permanent desirable changes in your life.

How to Make Your Affirmations Work for You

There are numerous ways of using affirmations:

- If you don't **BELIEVE** your affirmation, it won't work for you. If you are affirming that you are totally fit and healthy and you know you aren't fit and healthy, there's not much chance of a positive impact. If however you change it to the more believable, "I am now *willing* to improve my health," it will move you towards achieving your goal.

- If the affirmation is not supported by **ACTION**, you're wasting your time. If you are affirming how healthy you are while lying around eating junk food and watching television, the chances are that you'll never improve your health. If however you affirm this while going for a strenuous walk, you'll stand a better chance of succeeding.

- Work with one or more affirmation every day. The best times are just before sleeping, before starting the day and especially whenever you feel depressed or discouraged.

- Look in the mirror and say them to yourself out loud. Keep saying them until you eliminate all facial tension and grimaces and are able to see yourself with a relaxed happy expression.

- Another technique is to select an affirmation you want to concentrate on, write it down and then write down the negative thoughts that comes to mind as you think about it. Keep writing the affirmation over and over until no more negatives arise. Then turn each one of the negatives around into a positive statement that relates back to the affirmation you first chose.

- Say or write each affirmation in the first, second, and the third person. Always remember to put your own name in the affirmation and keep it in the present tense. Writing in the second and third person is also very important since your conditioning from others came to you in this manner.

- Continue working with the affirmations **DAILY** until they become totally integrated into your consciousness. You will know this when your mind responds positively and you begin to experience the desired results.

- Say them **OUT LOUD**. Hear them, take them in, experience them, and let them work for you.

- Record your affirmations and play them back on your iPod, phone, car system, etc.

- Sit across from a friend and repeat the affirmation out loud until you are comfortable doing so. Then have him/her say it to you in the second person. Your partner can observe your body language carefully. He/she should not let you go onto a new affirmation until you say the first one very clearly without contradictory body reactions (squirming, fidgeting, nervous laughing, etc.). Also he/she should continue to say it back to you in the second person until you can receive it confidently.

- Make your affirmations **VISIBLE**. Write them on cards and place them in highly visible areas. Place them on screen savers, desktops, your phone's welcome screen, etc.

The Way of the Tongue
How to Stay Positive and Boost Your Self-Esteem

How do you keep yourself and others positive especially in challenging times? How do you build and maintain your confidence when life can seem so difficult? Well… it all depends upon how you look at it.

A shoe factory sent two marketing scouts to a region in Africa to study the prospects for expanding business. One sent back a text saying, 'Situation hopeless, no one wears shoes'. The other sent a text saying, 'Glorious business opportunity, they have no shoes!' It all depends upon how you look at it.

What do you think of the following statement?	**Opportunitiesarenowhere**
What statement do you see?	**Opportunitiesarenowhere**
Is this what you see?	**Opportunities are nowhere**
Or is *this* what you see?	**Opportunities are now here**

It all depends upon how you look at it. But most people are **naturally inclined** to look at things in a certain way.

The Mind Is Like the Tongue

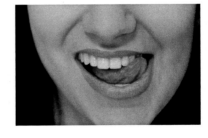

The mind is very much like the tongue in a way that it processes information. What do you do with your tongue? You move it around your mouth and examine your teeth *without even realising that you are doing so*. You are made conscious however when you discover a bit of stuck food or a rough edge. The tongue, like the mind, is continually looking for problems.

Think about it, your tongue doesn't stop until it finds something wrong. It doesn't take any notice of what is good. You never stop during this examination to say, "*Mmmm, that's a nice tooth, it's so smooth.*" No, like the mind, your tongue tends to look for and notice what is wrong, not what is right.

Being aware of this gives us an opportunity to do something about it. Most people are excellent trouble-shooters always on the lookout for flaws, faults, concerns, etc. Rather than appreciating all the good that is happening in their lives, they are constantly thinking of ways to improve their experience. A trouble-shooter can never really be satisfied because he or she is too busy evaluating life to enjoy it.

How do you Train Your Mind?

So if the natural tendency of the mind is to look for problems, what can you do about it? How can you train your mind? It is quite simple really. Get the tongue looking for and acknowledging the good teeth! Make yourself aware of all the wonderful, good, positive things in your life and express gratitude for them.

A Very Simple Exercise

Dedicate a few minutes every day to acknowledging what you have done well, what you are grateful for, and what you appreciate about your life. *Do it right now and see how it feels.*

What three things have you already done well today? Say them out loud.
1.
2.
3.

What are you grateful for?
1.
2.
3.
4.
5.
6.

How do you feel? If you can get yourself to focus on all the good things that you usually take for granted, you will build up a positive appreciation of healthy psychological functioning which will give you an inner-belief of strength and realistic balance, which is especially useful when times get tough. Invest a few minutes every day for a week acknowledging what you are grateful for and what you did well and I *bet* you'll make it an ongoing practice.

Start Your Team Meetings This Way

Why not begin each of your team meetings with, "*What have you done **well** in the last twenty-four hours?*"

Self-Esteem - Conditioning

We've been conditioned by others for many years. "*Who do you think you are?*" "*You should be ashamed of yourself*". And we add to this by being far too hard on ourselves. We worry and strive to improve our lives and in the process, often forget what we have achieved. We tend to forget or deny, or even feel embarrassed about admitting the things we do well. Here's another exercise to help build your self-esteem. Most of us have been taught that it's quite arrogant to boast. There is however a **big difference between thinking much about yourself and thinking about yourself so much**. Unless we have self-respect and think well of ourselves, how are we going to project confidence and enjoyment and inspire others? The following exercise has been designed to keep you in touch with your good side, to acknowledge your achievements, and to maintain a well-deserved feeling of self-esteem.

To begin the process, simply ask yourself the following questions and write down as many answers as possible. When you have completed the exercise, read through your list and add to it from time-to-time. Make a point of reading it especially when you feel low.

- What do I like about myself right now?

- What makes me unique?

- What have I achieved in my life?

- What am I proud of?

- What things have I failed to notice or appreciate about myself?

- What are the things I wouldn't want to change about myself?

- What am I grateful for?

- What do I have right now that I enjoy and am grateful for?

- What accomplishments have brought meaning to my life?

- What qualities and skills do I possess?

- What do others admire, respect, and like about me?

- Who are the people I am glad to have in my life.

- What else makes me happy?

- What are the main reasons that make me feel glad that I am who I am?

A Riddle for You

And finally………… Is this just another self-improvement idea that you've read which has left you thinking that one day you might try the exercise? Well then here's a riddle for you:

There were *five* birds sitting on a wire.

***Three* of them decided to fly away.**

How many birds were left on the wire?

The three only *decided* to fly away, they didn't get around to it (the answer is five). When all is said and done, much more is said than done! Take some time and put the ideas into action **now**.

Customer Service - Quality is not Enough
A Case for Survival!

The importance of providing excellent service in today's ever-changing, competitive marketplace cannot be overstated. Customers have become ever more discerning and demanding and now that social media has revolutionised Word-of-Mouth, poor service is exposed almost immediately and can cripple a company very quickly.

The quality of customer service can be affected by cumbersome policies, poor systems, staffing levels, etc., but understanding what customers really need is the quickest and easiest way of ensuring you stay in business.

Two Different Types of Needs

Customers judge service by two different types of needs - Practical and Personal. A company's ability to meet a customer's Practical Needs in today's fast-changing, technological market is taken for granted. If a company does not have a *quality* product or service, it will be difficult for them to stay in business. Excellent service however, is the factor that makes the difference. Today's customers are not only seeking quality to fulfil their Practical Needs, they also have Personal Needs; they are seeking reliability, trust, attention, and the respect they deserve.

"Profit in business comes from repeat customers, customers that boast about your project or service, and customers that bring friends with them." *W. Edwards Deming*

Practical Needs

Businesses need to be able to provide products and services that meet their customers' specific practical needs.

**"Quality in a service or product is not what you put into it.
It is what the client or customer gets out of it."** *Peter Drucker*

Personal Needs

The fulfilment of Practical Needs is not enough to keep customers satisfied. A Personal Need refers to how customers like to be treated and spoken to, and especially how they *feel* about how they have been treated.

Meeting only one of these needs is not good enough. Imagine going for a haircut and the assistant keeps you waiting; is blunt and impersonal and then (if you hadn't walked out yet), gives you an excellent haircut. They've met your *Practical Needs* but have completely ignored your *Personal Needs*.

Consider the opposite - As you enter the premises you are greeted with a smile; they remember your name; offer you a cup of tea; maintain friendly eye-contact; listen carefully to what you want, and overall make you feel very welcome. Then they give you a 'nightmare' haircut. Both *Practical* and *Personal Needs* must be met.

"A satisfied customer is the best business strategy of all." *Michael LeBoeuf*

What Do People Mean?

People often refer to service as being good or bad. To understand what people mean when they refer to the level of customer service received, think back to a time when you, as a customer, received *excellent service* and make a list of what the person did or said that made you perceive the service as excellent. You will probably be surprised at the absolute simplicity of the actions taken. Typically, people have said:

- *He greeted me.*
- *She said she would call me and she did.*
- *He said they would deliver by four and they did.*
- *He took time to listen to me.*
- *She thanked me.*
- *They were cheerful and reasonably quick.*
- *He looked up the address for me.*
- *He took the time to explain the details to me.*
- *She showed me how it worked.*

Considering your personal experience of good customer service, ask yourself how you think the person who served you felt about their job. Almost always the answer is positive. It's amazing how many organisations just don't see the connection between providing excellent customer service and creating job satisfaction and high morale.

**"It is not the employer who pays the wages. Employers only handle the money.
It is the customer who pays the wages."** *Henry Ford*

Now repeat the process but this time with a *poor* customer service experience. List the specific actions that were, or were not taken when you received bad service, in other words, describe what a person did or said that made you think the service was bad. When you have completed your list, gauge the impact on the company by answering the following questions:

- How did you feel after the transaction?
- Have you gone back to that organisation?
- Have you told other people about your experience?
- Have you posted any details of your experience on Facebook, Twitter or on a Review Site?
- How do you think the person who served you felt during and after the interaction?
- Do you think that person enjoyed his or her job?

"Your most unhappy customers are your greatest source of learning." *Bill Gates*

So What Is Customer Service?

Having examined the impact of good and bad service, it's important to understand what excellent customer service is and how to provide it. You can measure everything you and your staff do, including your systems, paperwork, policies, etc., against the following definition:

Customer service is
Everything you do and say
That makes every Customer feel
Welcome, Important and Comfortable

Everything:	No exceptions.
You:	*Your* contribution, your responsibility.
Do and say:	In whichever way you communicate with customers.
That makes *every* customer feel:	No exceptions and this includes internal customers as well.
Welcome:	Every time they phone, log on, walk in the door, etc.
Important:	Give each individual customer your *total* attention.
Comfortable:	Consider how each customer wants to be treated.

Are You Ready?

Select your customer-facing staff carefully. Train them in good interpersonal skills and ensure that all senior personnel model the required behaviours.

"You have a much better chance of achieving good service values
if you treat your staff the way you would like them to treat your customers." *Russ Baleson*

The specific actions that exemplify good service are almost always relatively simple actions that are quick and easy to perform. It would be worth your while to make a list of simple actions or ideas that you could put into practice to ensure that you provide consistently good service to your customers. Even better would be to ask your staff to suggest and commit to these actions.

"Do what you do so well that they will want to see it again and bring their friends." *Walt Disney*

Goalsetting - Getting Through the Motivation Dip

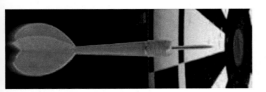

There is much to be said about the psychology and the structure of effective goal-setting, but this section focuses on a technique to help you through the motivation dip that occurs quite soon after setting goals.

What Is The Motivation Dip?

One of the reasons people don't succeed in achieving their goals is because of the effects of the Motivation Dip. When choosing a new goal, one's motivation is quite high but somehow, over time, it doesn't last.

Think about what happens when a person takes up a new sport or hobby or begins a new project. At first they are so motivated that they can't talk about anything else except for their new gained enthusiasm. For example when someone joins a gym the motivation gained from actually going to the gym, getting some exercise, feeling a slight physical difference very quickly, is motivating. This is the 'Novelty Phase'.

Then after a while, after some time has elapsed, the novelty wears off and it's replaced by the need for hard work, which could mean getting out of bed earlier or resisting any of the temptations that take us away from the goal. It is at this stage that most people experience a real dip in their motivation level and become discouraged. The dieter starts to overeat again, the person who chose to study gets the urge to spend the evening watching television instead, and the athlete can't summon up the energy to go out and exercise. Sound familiar?

If you can just get through this difficult dip until you begin to achieve tangible results, then the results themselves will act as a motivator to sustain your actions.

You should be formulating your goals in such a way so that even when you're at the bottom of the Motivation Dip, the benefits of the goal are so clear that it entices you to keep going. Then as soon as you experience significant results your motivation rises again.

Also your goals must be written in such a way that they help to crystallise your thoughts, and those thoughts will help motivate the action required. Overall, goals need to be specific; positive (focus on what you want, not on what you don't want); observable action (what can I see myself doing when I've achieved the goal?); realistic and attainable; and a challenge.

Anchoring

But back to what this section is all about - a technique to help sustain your motivation to achieve your goals. This technique is called Anchoring. Firstly, let's examine a simple way to set up a 'calm' anchor to help you in times of stress, anxiety, worry, etc., and then how to use the same technique to support your goals.

Setting up a Calm Anchor

You can 'anchor' feelings to a specific part of your body. Once this anchor is established you can recall and sometimes relive the feelings by pressing that spot on your body that serves as a TRIGGER for these feelings. This technique merely uses the mind's natural talent for linking things together and making associations.

The process of making associations usually happens without our conscious awareness. It is an everyday occurrence. For example, if you were to hear a song that you used to listen to many years ago, it could automatically trigger off a flood of memories about what you were experiencing at that time. The following exercise should only take about five to ten minutes and shows you how you can use associations to set up your very own calm anchor.

The Process

- Allow yourself to RELAX, feel comfortable and close your eyes. Use whatever process works for you; breathing exercises, individual muscle tension and release, etc.

- Think of a time and place in your life when you felt really calm, confident and relaxed. IMAGINE yourself in that place. Immerse yourself in that experience, making it as real as possible by exploring that place with all your senses. SEE all the surroundings and colours and light and shades and textures. HEAR all the different sounds and the way that they seem to blend with one another. Notice all the pleasant SMELLS of the place. TOUCH the surroundings and experience what they feel like. Use your sense of TASTE if appropriate. Allow your breathing to become slow and deep.

- When you feel the relaxation of that experience in your body and mind, ANCHOR it to a certain part of your body; for instance let your thumbnail dig into the pad of your first finger.

- HOLD the anchor long enough to allow the association between the touch and the relaxed feelings to occur, about TWENTY SECONDS, then release the anchor.

- Then TEST THE ANCHOR and continuously strengthen the association with ongoing repetition.

Once the anchor is established, anytime you feel stressed or anxious, touch the spot in the same way with the same pressure and notice how you can recall or relive the pleasant relaxing and calming feelings. It is best to use the technique as soon as you feel the slightest twinge of anxiety and stop it before it has the chance to make you feel uncomfortable.

An Anchor to Support Your Goal

You can also use an anchor to support your goals to ensure you make it through the Motivation Dip. The following exercise should take about thirty minutes.

Close your eyes and take some time to allow yourself to relax. Imagine that you have achieved a specific goal to your total satisfaction. Immerse yourself in all the benefits and joys of such an achievement making it as real as possible and exploring the experience with all your senses. Then ask yourself:

- What do I see? - See and experience all the positive motivating results.
- How do I feel? - Feel all the associated wonderful, powerful, feelings.
- What do I feel? - Feel all the physical sensations. Touch your success.
- What do I hear? - Hear all the positive sounds and voices.
- What do I smell? - Experience it.
- How is my body physically different? - Feel it.
- What do I taste? - Experience it.
- What am I wearing? - See it, feel it, be comfortable and motivated in it.
- What am I saying to myself? - Say it, hear it, feel good!
- What am I saying to others? - Say it, hear it, see others react positively.
- What are others saying to me? - Hear it, see how supportive and happy they are.
- What are others saying about me? - Hear it, see how supportive and happy they all are.
- What impact will I have on others? - See it, hear it, feel it, experience it.
- What else is positively different? - Experience it.

When you feel the magic of the goal-achieving experience in your body and mind, **ANCHOR** it to a certain part of your body; for instance gently press your thumb nail into the side of your first finger.

HOLD the anchor long enough to allow the association between the touch and the feelings of achievement, about twenty seconds, and then release the anchor. Then **TEST** the Anchor and continuously strengthen the association with ongoing repetition.

Trigger

So, quite simply, every time you feel a bit lazy or begin to rationalise as to why you'll take action at some later date, or why just this once, you'll ...... (do what you don't really want to do), press your trigger and let all the benefits of sticking to your goal come flooding back through all your senses.

The Clock is Ticking!
A Lesson in Time Management

A trip to the U.S.A. I was one of seven thousand delegates at the American Society for Training and Development annual conference in Atlanta. It had been an overwhelmingly informative week, fast-moving, challenging, and I felt worn out.

I was standing outside the Peachtree Plaza Hotel with about seven other people, none of whom I knew, waiting for transport to the airport. I couldn't wait to get to New York. After working at a very fast pace for a long time, I had scheduled four days of holiday and even though I was feeling weary, I was excited about all the things I had planned to do in New York. Looking around, I noticed that the people waiting for the airport shuttle had also attended the ASTD conference. They looked worn out too. And that's when I met Eddie.

Eddie was the shuttle driver and his mini-bus was spotless. He reminded me of the Basketball legend, Michael Jordan. He was tall, skinny, and moved with vibrant energy.

"How're you all doin'?" he asked, looking directly at us and grinning as if he was really enjoying himself. "All for the airport?" he asked while he opened the back of the mini-bus to load the luggage.

He very quickly introduced himself and at the same time took note of our luggage and enquired about each person's specific airport terminal. When he got to me he extended his hand and said, "Hi, I'm Eddie and you are?" "I'm Russ, Eddie", I said shaking his hand, "Terminal two please and these are my bags".

"Thanks Russ". From that moment on, whenever Eddie addressed any of us, (which he did often), he addressed us by name. He proceeded to load our cases taking into account the way they would be offloaded. As he was doing so he grinned at us and said, "Hey, we all have something in common." I was affected by his open and energetic manner and so I asked, "What Eddie, what do we have in common?" "We all hate carrying this luggage!" A few people laughed. "But let me explain", he said. "This luggage is a little heavier than it should be. Little, so-called samples of soap or slippers that are provided by the hotel that were just too tempting perhaps?"

"Ha! Got you Bev and you too Arthur," he offered with a smile to the two people who had decided to examine their shoes rather than maintain eye-contact. By the time we boarded, people were chatting and laughing and the atmosphere was much more alive than it had been. I was amazed. I loved this guy. How did he do it? He was a shuttle driver on a hot afternoon and he was having fun. What energy!

"Well folks, at no extra charge and only a few minutes extra and I could take you past the big stadium they're building for the Games. It's really awesome. Wanna see it?" We all agreed and he became our friendly tour guide.

At one point in the journey, we were held up in some traffic and I took the opportunity to find out more about him. "How do you do it Eddie?"

"How do I do what Russ?" I was still amazed at how he remembered and used everyone's name. I felt as if we had known one-another for years. "How do you keep so positive, so alive, how do you keep so passionate about everything you do?"

I was sitting behind him and I will never forget the power of his message. He turned around, looked directly into my eyes and said, "This is my life Russ! My life doesn't start when I get home. My life doesn't start when I'm back home with my family. It doesn't start on Friday evening…. Or when the children have left school… Or when I finally achieve some of the goals I've been working on." He lifted his hand and tapped the glass on his wrist-watch with two fingers. "The clock is ticking.   NOW!"

I don't really remember the rest of the journey. I sat there enjoying the realisation of wisdom. There I had been, waiting to get to New York so that I could have some fun. Eddie was having fun now, even while he worked. The clock is *always* ticking. I had been almost oblivious to my surroundings other than those that Eddie had been pointing out. I wasn't taking the time to live in the present moment.

Thank you Eddie. This is now an integral part of my values and whenever I lose track of it, I clearly see your eyes, locking on mine, "This is my life!" The clock *is* ticking and now, even after all these years, one of my favourite affirmations that I've borrowed from my daughter is, "You have to have some fun *every* day!"

"It is not uncommon for people to spend their whole life waiting to start living." *Eckhart Tolle*

"Time isn't precious at all, because it is an illusion. What you perceive as precious is not time but the one point that is out of time: the Now. That is precious indeed. The more you are focused on time - past and future - the more you miss the Now, the most precious thing there is." *Eckhart Tolle*

Self-Coaching
And a Blind Coaching Exercise for Managers

Here is a simple, yet powerful coaching process, to help you gain insight into any issue. It can also be used by managers or team leaders as a 'Blind Coaching' session facilitated for groups of people.

A Self-Coaching Process

Set aside a quiet space where you won't be interrupted for at least fifteen minutes, and quite simply, read each of the questions on the next page and write down the answers that *immediately* come to mind. Each question has been formulated to help you gain insight into how to proceed with something that is causing some level of frustration or hasn't quite worked for you. The process is typical of that followed by most Coaches and isn't intended to replace a one-to-one coaching discussion. It's merely a method to help you find a direction when you aren't sure of the way forward.

Choose a goal or an issue that is affecting you at the moment and simply write down the answers to the questions on the following page. There is no short-cut. It's important that you actually *write* (or type if you must) the answers in full to create the necessary awareness.

A Facilitated Process

Using the same list of questions, a Manager or Team Leader can facilitate a session to achieve a variety of objectives.

- Explain the objective of the exercise - for example, to experience the power of effective coaching questions / to help identify a way of proceeding with an individual or group issue, etc. Explain that no feedback will be required from the delegates during the exercise.

- The issue to be selected can be approached in different ways. You could ask delegates to choose the concern that is the biggest challenge they face at that moment. You could ask them to choose something very personal that would not require sharing, or something that could be shared to benefit the group as well as the individual.

- In some circumstances, *you* could provide the focus - a group problem, a goal, target, challenge, etc.
- Once you have chosen and explained the format of the session, ask the delegates to choose the focus as appropriate.
- Use the questions listed on the next page as a guide, or ask other relevant Coaching Questions over a period of approximately fifteen minutes to coach delegates through the process. When complete, facilitate accordingly.

Coaching Questions

- What is the issue you would like to work on?

- What effect does it have?

- What would you like to achieve?

- What would be *really* good about achieving it?

- How will you know you've achieved it?

- What specifically do you want to achieve from this exercise during the next fifteen minutes?

- What have you done so far to address this issue?

- What has worked?

- What hasn't worked?

- What haven't you been doing?

- Why haven't you solved it yet?

- Which parts are within your control?

- What could you do?

- What have you seen work?

- What would you do if you were ten years younger?

- If someone you knew and respected was in the exact same position regarding this issue, what might they do?

- Think of someone you admire and respect, anyone at all that would have experience in dealing with this issue. Imagine you asked them for advice on this issue. What do you think they might say?

- What would happen if you did nothing?

- Of all the options so far which one interests you most?

- What are you going to do?

- What is the specific first action you *will* take and exactly when will that be?

- On a scale of one to ten, how confident are you are that you *will* be doing this?

- If your rating is less than ten, what *will* you do to increase it?

- Rate, out of ten, how far you've moved forward on this issue since you started this exercise.

When All Is Said and Done..........
When all is said and done, a lot more is said than done!

Unless you take action, this has been a waste of time. After gaining insight from the coaching process, don't think of what you *could, would, should, might, must*, or will *try* to do. Decide on *at least* one specific action, one thing that you definitely *will* be doing.

Transfer at least one action that you will be taking into your diary. Ensure that the action is specific, in other words, it describes:

- What you will actually be doing.
- How you will be doing it.
- How well you will be doing it.
- When you will be doing it.
- When you will have completed it.
- How you will know when you have been successful.
- What support you might need from others to achieve it.

**"Action may not always bring happiness,
but there is no happiness
without action."**
Benjamin Disraeli

Difficult Conversations for Managers

Handling difficult conversations is one of the more challenging parts of a manager's role. It is relatively easy to deliver a difficult message and leave a person feeling de-motivated, but it takes skill, gravitas and diplomacy to deliver it whilst maintaining self-esteem and motivation.

If your intention is to support the individual and/or improve performance, you can use the following structure to deliver your message effectively.

1. **Set the Agenda - What and Why.**
2. **Ask For Their Input.**
3. **Listen To Understand.**
4. **Make Expectations Clear.**
5. **Close The Loop / Discuss Next Steps.**

1. Set the Agenda - What and Why

Open the discussion by briefly and simply stating WHAT (*the observable behaviour*) you want to talk to them about and WHY you want to talk to them about it. This sets the agenda and the tone for the meeting right from the outset. For example: "*I'd like to talk to you about some of the remarks you made about customers in the team meeting yesterday because I was concerned about the impression you made on some of the new people.*"

2. Ask For Their Input

It's important that you ask them to explain their point of view or reasons for their behaviour before taking the discussion any further. For example: "*Could you tell me why this happened?*" or, "*I'd like to understand your point of view on this.*"

3. Listen to Understand

It is pointless asking them for their input if you aren't going to listen to them. Listening with the *intention* of understanding their perceptions, reasons, motivation, etc., will provide you with the substance you need to take the discussion further (or not).

Most people listen from their own perspective, in other words, from a point of 'How does this affect me?' We need to strive to understand the other person's point of view, to listen from *their* perspective, not ours. How is what they are saying affecting *them*? How are *they* feeling about what they are saying? If your intention is focused on their perspective and you are trying to understand what they are saying, you will really be listening and will have the substance required to take the most appropriate action.

4. Make Expectations Clear

The purpose of these discussions is to improve behaviour rather than to punish it. Make your expectations *crystal* clear at this stage and check that they fully understand the *specific behaviour* that's required of them in the future. Most of the time we assume that expectations are crystal clear because they seem to be common sense. But just because it's crystal clear to you doesn't mean it is to anyone else. The easiest way to check if your expectations are clear is to ask yourself, "*If someone else asked that person what they think I expected them to do in a certain situation, what would they say? What would their actual words be?*"

5. Close the Loop / Discuss the Next Steps

Depending upon the situation and the circumstances, the action you take in this step can vary considerably. Sometimes no further action is necessary other than you reinforcing their behaviour with appropriate feedback at a later stage. It might be necessary however to schedule a follow-up meeting or to make them aware of the consequences that will follow if their behaviour does not change to the required standards.

Once Upon A Time
The Power of Storytelling

How do you engage the hearts and minds of your audience? How do you grab attention away from the myriad thoughts running through their minds? How do you get them to grasp and then remember the intention of your message? Presenting, facilitating, training, and teaching all offer the same challenge.

Children at a very young age learn to listen, fantasise and relate to lessons within entertaining tales. Ancient philosophers and religious leaders used parables (stories) to teach and influence. Many years ago, psychotherapists told stories about monsters and dragons in order for their patients to be able to face their fears in a symbolic and safe way. Folk stories, passed down through the times are *still* told and sung, and convey a definite message that is easy to remember.

Yes, storytelling is a powerful tool to help you touch your audience. Good stories gain attention and help people to understand the link between the lesson and their own lives. They are a way of establishing common ground between you and your audience and motivating them without risking intimidation. People easily relate because they can make the connection with their situation far better than anyone else can. They don't feel threatened by someone pushing ideas on to them and therefore interpret and learn the message at their own pace, in their own way.

Good trainers and presenters are instinctive storytellers. They realise that a form of entertainment is required - the skill of engaging the audience with relevant and helpful analogies. Without this, a presentation or speech is just a dump of information.

Our senses are very powerful memory triggers. You may hear a song that you last heard twenty years ago and immediately recall the smell of the perfume, the emotions of being with your dancing partner, the lights of the party, the taste of the food, etc. The sounds of the song trigger memories that recall other senses and details to mind. Stories do that too.

Careful though! Stories without connection or context are worse than no stories at all. The best anecdotes come from your own life experiences. If you relate a tale that doesn't remind you of an experience you've had, it's bound to sound hollow and fake. As soon as something touches your life, you have a new story. Don't worry about having to be too accurate with your stories; they can be improved by a little embroidery, but only use stories you embroider. To touch others, you must be touched!

- Use genuine, personal stories that have meaning for you.

- Link the story to the objective you are trying to achieve. This is important! Know exactly why you are telling it and how it links to that specific audience.

- Get your emotions and body into the story. Act it out and enjoy yourself.

- Be vivid. Choose words that paint a picture, describe sounds, and involve feelings and other senses. These emotive details make it real for the listeners.

That reminds me of a time when………………

I Understand How You Feel
Challenging the Paradigm of How to Communicate Empathy

Understanding a Person's Condition from *Their* Perspective

Empathy - from Greek empatheia (from em-'in' + pathos 'feeling'). People often confuse the words *Empathy* and *Sympathy*. Empathy is the experience of understanding another person's condition from their perspective whereas Sympathy means feelings of pity and sorrow for someone else's misfortune.

Challenging the Paradigm

A paradigm is a theory or belief system that guides the way we do things. It can be defined as a pattern or model; a set of assumptions, concepts, values, and practices that constitute a way of viewing reality. It's easy to buy into a paradigm when it seems logical and you have no other frame of reference. It isn't however always the wisest thing to do. This article challenges the paradigm of how to communicate or respond with empathy.

Where does it Begin?

When people listen, they do so naturally from their own perspective. The concept of responding with empathy begins with the intention of understanding the other person's point of view from *their* perspective, not one's own. How is what they are saying affecting *them*? How do you imagine *they* are feeling about what they are saying? Communication is driven by intention, not technique so be clear on your intention when you are listening and responding with empathy.

I Understand How You Feel. (Oh No You Don't!)

How do you feel when somebody tells you that they understand how you feel? Most of the time it's annoying even though the person might be genuinely empathic.

We have learned to communicate empathy in some strange ways. We have been taught to imagine how we would feel if we were in a similar position to someone else and this would help us to empathise with them. If you were to empathise by asking yourself, "How would I feel if I was that person?" you have missed the point. It really isn't about you at all.

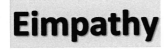

What is it about the word Eimpathy? Did you notice the incorrect spelling? There is no 'i' in Empathy and *that is the key*. When you put yourself in someone else's shoes you are typically trying to imagine how you would feel if you were in that person's place. But there is no 'i' in Empathy. In other words, this is not about you, this is about them.

Listen First

You can't respond with empathy unless you have been listening with empathy. In other words, you first need to listen and try to understand how they are feeling before you can respond appropriately. Instead of saying, "I understand how you feel, it happened to me too," simply consider how you think *they* are feeling and check it out. For example, "You seem to be quite *worried* about how long it is taking?"

When responding with empathy, remember to relate back both *the* FEELING and the CONTENT to the other person. For example, *"You must be feeling very frustrated* (feeling) *that you didn't get there on time?"* (content)

In our quest to help, we often rush to give advice or suggest a course of action when most of the time providing empathy would be far more appropriate. Some people compound matters even further by using the irritating phrase, "If I were you I would….." Always check if someone wants advice before giving it to them.

Here are some more examples of responding with empathy.

- You seem to be *concerned* about how it will impact on your customers?
- You seem quite *excited* about meeting your nephew?
- It must be *frustrating* not having enough time to complete the project?
- You must be *annoyed* that he didn't consult you first?
- You seem *disappointed* that they didn't use your design?
- You seem quite *sad* that he's gone?
- You seem *delighted* that you no longer have to work in that office?
- You seem *relieved* that he finally saw your point of view?

Connecting With Others

Listening with empathy and responding appropriately is one of the most powerful techniques you can use to develop your communication skills and improve your relationships. Being understood is a fundamental psychological need that we all have. A well communicated empathic response will clearly show the other person that you are sincere and that you *do* understand. Take time to listen to understand, and experience an immediate positive impact.

The Gospel According to Them
They say that ……………..

Do you believe in old wives' tales, urban legends, proverbs, superstition, folklore, etc.? It seems so easy to buy into them without question, but is this wise?

Imagine this...

A tall, old-fashioned glass-faced building in the town of Victim Regis housed the offices of **Them**. The large conference room was furnished neatly but without taste. The carpet was one shade of green, the walls another. The dark wooden table dominated most of the room and the bookcases and the three or four-hundred volumes in them looked tattered and used.

A large plaque displaying the words, **THE ROOM OF THEY** stood next to a few aged, skeletal typewriters.

The table was covered in papers. These were being moved around in some kind of logical order so that all appeared at least once before each of the thirty-three committee members sitting around the table making affirmative and often unconscious noises. Most of the papers contained only brief sentences and a few of them, pushed to the extreme left corner, bore twenty, rather messy looking signatures. The walls were decorated with 'Their' successes. These were the papers that had been approved and published for distribution and *had changed the lives and thinking patterns of people everywhere.*

All of them were prefaced with the words, **'THEY SAY THAT…..'**

- It's got to get worse before it gets better.
- If there is no pain there is no gain.
- Bad things happen in threes.
- Rules are rules.
- A bird in the hand is worth two in the bush.
- An apple a day keeps the doctor away.
- Pride comes before a fall.
- Carrots improve your vision.
- You must feed a cold and starve a fever.
- A man who owes no money is a rich man.
- A poor excuse is better than none at all.
- Practice makes perfect.
- You don't need tonsils.
- You don't need an appendix.
- You should keep your elbows off the table.

- There is a bug going around.
- Breakfast is the most important meal of the day.
- You must drink sixteen glasses of water a day to be healthy.
- One day when you grow up….
- You mustn't swim on a full stomach.
- You must respect your elders.
- Sugar gives you go.
- Men are all the same.
- You can't teach an old dog new tricks.

I've taught new tricks to many 'old dogs' and laugh at some of the things I used to believe. Some of the affirmations we live by have come to us in the form of quotations, idioms, proverbs, and sayings and we have allowed them to influence and shape our thinking. You can however *choose* the affirmations that you want to shape your life. How many of the above (and others) do you unconsciously buy into? Do you borrow other people's thoughts and fears? Are you choosing your thoughts and beliefs consciously? Well, they say that........ No! Wait a minute, there is no They!

When to Coach and When Not to Coach?

When, where, and in what circumstances is coaching appropriate? Here are some of the more obvious opportunities to apply coaching at work:

- Motivating people.
- Delegating.
- Problem solving.
- Relationship issues.
- Team building.
- Appraisals and assessments.
- Task performance.
- Planning and reviewing.
- Self-development.

The list is endless and the opportunities can be tackled by using either a highly-structured coaching session or a much less formal approach.

It's more important however to be aware of the underlying principles of coaching during the various interactions that occur on a daily basis. These might not require formal coaching but rather an appropriate coaching style of management: For example:

Sue is working on a task that had been discussed and agreed with her manager. She now has a problem and goes to discuss this with her manager:

Sue: I did what we agreed and it isn't working.

Manager: Okay, try it this way instead.

               No coaching there, but consider the following alternative, based on the coaching principles of creating Awareness and Responsibility.

Sue: I did what we agreed and it isn't working.

Manager: Okay, I'm off to a meeting right now. See if you can find out exactly where and when the problem occurs, and I'll be back to help you find a solution.

               Ten minutes later when the manager returns:

Sue: I've got the solution, it is working fine now.

Manager: Great, what did you do?

Sue: This was the problem, and I got around it like this…… There are no other effects, I've checked that out.

Manager: Good thinking, and well done for checking the effects, that means we can let Marketing know it's ready for implementation.

When is Coaching Less Appropriate?

Delivering a reprimand or even confirming a standard will usually require a much more direct approach with a lower level of involvement. For example, a manager would begin by explaining what they wanted to talk about (a specific behaviour that they have found inappropriate) and the reason that they need to have the discussion. After listening to the reason for behaving in such a way, the manager would then reinforce the behavioural expectations required in the future and if appropriate, the consequences of a reoccurrence. Depending upon the circumstances, this would be an appropriately direct way of approaching this type of interaction.

Coaching is not merely a technique to be rigidly wheeled out and applied in certain prescribed circumstances. It is a way of managing, a way of treating people, a way of thinking, a way of being.

"Coaching is about unlocking a person's potential to maximise their own performance. It is helping them to learn rather than teaching them." *Timothy Gallwey*

When to Coach? It All Depends

And so back to the question, "When to coach?" The reason this question often presents a dilemma is because of the way the question is asked. Instead of asking, *"When should I coach?"* you would get far more insight if you asked:

- When do I use a coaching approach in a conversation?
- When is it appropriate to get someone more involved in a conversation?
- When do I need to get someone more engaged in a discussion?
- When should I use more of a Pull Style of Communication in a discussion?
- When is it appropriate to get someone to think through a situation rather than providing the answers for them?
- When is it appropriate to use a one-way approach?
- When is it appropriate to use a two-way approach?

The answers to most of these questions is that *it all depends* upon your intention, the subject under discussion, the person's ability and knowledge of the topic being discussed, etc. In other words, it is very flexible and the approach needs to be considered to match the situation at hand. The level of engagement might even change several times in one discussion!

For example, a manager facilitating a training workshop could be asked a question and instead of answering it, chooses to engage the delegates in order for them to think through the answer for themselves (*a coaching style to create Awareness and Responsibility*). So the discussion might take the form of:

Delegate: What is the best way to motivate a consultant who is already performing well?

Manager: Have you got any particular consultant in mind? (*coaching*)

Delegate: Yes, three of them.

Manager: What are you trying at the moment? (*coaching*)

Delegate: Well I've tried to ………………

Manager: And how has that worked? (*coaching*)

Delegate: We've been able to……….

Manager: And what else has worked? (*coaching*)

Delegate: Approaching it as if ………….

Manager: And what have you tried that hasn't worked? (*coaching*)

Delegate: I've tried to ………………

Manager: And what other options are open to you? (*coaching*)

Delegate: I guess I could …………. and ……………………..

Manager: (*To all the delegates*) Does anyone else have any ideas of the best way to motivate these consultants? (*coaching*)

Delegates: Yes, you could …………………or you could even ………………

Manager: (*To original questioner*): Which of all of these do you think will add the most value? (*coaching*)

Delegate: Definitely asking them to …………………

Manager: Good, let me know the outcome. There is a lot of good thinking and insight here. I think that the best approach is always to consider each individual separately rather than trying to motivate all top performers with the same approach. (*Reinforcing a good action and helping to provide an answer*).

Levels of Involvement

So in summary, when deciding when to coach, consider the level of involvement appropriate at the time.

The purpose of coaching is to involve or engage the person in order to increase their awareness, responsibility and self-belief. To do this, adjust your style to the individual, the situation, and the task and also to each response you receive in the conversation. And whilst doing this, be careful not to interrupt their thought process and answers.

If we could just stop ourselves from responding too quickly and keep quiet for a while after the person has responded, we would promote awareness and responsibility. And that is coaching!

Telephone Prospecting

The part of selling that many people dislike and consequently battle through every time, is prospecting for new clients by telephone. It all sounds so simple. Just phone the prospect and get an appointment to see them. Not so easy in practice, or is it?

The first thing to do is to acknowledge that you are in the marketing business. Unless you actively and regularly talk to potential clients, you have little chance of making a success of your business.

Making appointments with prospects can be nerve-racking, difficult and at times even de-motivating. But there are techniques that will make this challenge much easier and certainly more effective.

Identifying Your Target Market

The place to start is by correctly identifying your target market. If you do gain an appointment but find that your products or services are inappropriate, you have wasted your time. The following is a simple technique to enable you to identify suitable prospects. Take time to answer the following questions in detail:

- Describe the type of customer that your product or service typically appeals to.
- Where are these customers usually situated?
- What type of Industry is your product or service most suited to?
- Who would be the right person to contact? (What position does the *decision-maker* hold?)

Planning

Once you have identified your customer profile, you can use several on-line resources that often include maps of the area to help you locate prospective clients. It is then time for background work. Look at your own company records to check if you have ever dealt with the prospect in the past or are even dealing with them at present. To ensure that the call will be worthwhile, do some background research about the company's history, size, locations, strategy, values, products, people, etc., before trying to gain an appointment.

Time Management and Discipline

Prospecting is a structured activity. Set an objective to make a specific number of calls and don't stop until you have achieved them. During this time, ensure that no calls are put through to you, clear your desk of all other work and give this task your complete attention. Beware of flimsy rationalisation! It is easy to justify delays in getting started, after all, this work has been uncomfortable in the past.

Strategy and Structuring Your Call

The strategy required for gaining an appointment is *very different* to that of face-to-face selling skills. You cannot sell a high-value product or service over the telephone. Your main objective at this stage is to *get the appointment*, not to sell your product or service. You can safely assume that your prospect normally screens many calls from salespeople as part of a daily routine and so your call has to be professional, brief, assertive, and most of all, convincing. The following three-step strategy will help you to increase your rate of success.

1. Introduce yourself and your company
Confidently ask for your prospect by name, not by designation. Take the time to identify who you will be speaking to before you make the call. Introduce yourself and the company you represent clearly and briefly. It will help if you can mention a credible source of reference at this stage.

2. State the reason for your call
How will the prospect benefit by seeing you? Confidently provide a valid reason before asking for the appointment. For example, you might say, "We have an exciting new development that has been especially designed for your industry's marketing needs."

3. Ask for an appointment
Your main objective is to get an appointment and to do this you'll have to use assertive closing techniques. For example, you could say, "I'm going to be in your area on Thursday and Friday, which day would suit you best?" When suggesting a convenient time to meet, give the prospect two alternatives and if neither one is suitable, ask for another.

Objections
If you are faced with an objection, and this is going to happen from time to time, keep trying until you get the appointment. Above all, don't underestimate the power of the personal assistant and the typical role that this person plays. It is their function to shield the boss from unnecessary calls. Your manner should be warm and professional and at the same time persuasive. Don't settle for sending brochures or e-mailing information. The chances are that you will never hear from them again. You have to gain an appointment or you have failed. When you are gaining more appointments than you are losing, then consider yourself successful.

Summary
Don't try and sell high-value goods and services on the phone. Your objective is to gain the appointment and you will need to sound professional, interesting and most of all, persuasive. Remember too, that referrals are a much easier way of gaining new business and this is usually only obtained by developing and nurturing long-term business relationships based on trust.

Expert Product Knowledge for Salespeople

Product or service knowledge is vital to a salesperson's effectiveness. Without it they lack credibility and confidence. Salespeople should be held accountable for being experts in their profession and staying informed of all product and service innovations; changes; and competitor information.

If salespeople are spoon-fed product knowledge, much of the impact and retention are undermined and it also causes a lack of initiative when products are updated or new ones are introduced. Of course the company should assist in the process but their challenge lies in:

- How to assist without taking away responsibility.
- How to maintain a professional representation of the company's products and services.
- How to make it easy for salespeople to keep abreast of new technology; new products and services; competitor information; ever-changing customer needs; market trends, etc.

How to Learn Product Knowledge

The answer lies in the way that salespeople *learn* product knowledge. It was a Mr E. K. Strong who in the 1920's recognised a way of presenting merchandise that proved to be more persuasive than others. This is called the **FAB** approach - the **F**eatures, **A**dvantages and **B**enefits analysis of service and products which when used properly, makes the task of learning about products and selling them much easier.

The FAB strategy is quite common in the Selling and Marketing profession but over many years has been misinterpreted and changed from the original concept. For example, the 'Advantage' in FAB has been dropped by many. This completely undermines the value and effectiveness of this tried and tested method.

Written Word - Spoken Word

Most salespeople get their product information from websites, brochures, product packaging and memos from their marketing department. These are usually learned 'parrot-fashion' without the necessary understanding of how to communicate it to customers. One of the problems within sales-communication is the fact that the written word and the spoken word are very different. It would be quite normal for a product brochure to state, 'So you can be assured of its continued, structural strength'. But try to imagine yourself using those exact words when speaking to a customer!

The Best Way?

There are many ways of obtaining product knowledge but the method that is the most logical and proves to be effective in the long-term is: *To learn the product knowledge in the same way that you will be communicating the information.* In other words, structure your knowledge session so that it links directly with the way you'll be presenting the information to the customer.

Where do you start? The principle of effective and persuasive selling is: Meet your customer's need with a Benefit Statement. So let us have a closer look at FAB which is an effective way to learn, understand and communicate product knowledge to customers.

Feature - *A Feature is a characteristic of a product or service.*

All products and all services have features. Characteristics that describe what they are. It's that simple. Features will always answer the question, "What is it?" or "What does it have?"

For example:
- *It has a five-year guarantee.*
- *It is £899-00.*
- *It has a built-in Anti-Virus protection programme.*

Advantage

Imagine 'spraying' your customer with lots of Features and 'praying' that some of them were relevant. You would also need to pray that your customer understood what each one was and how it contributed to his or her needs. This is another common error made by many salespeople. It's called, *'The Spray and Pray Method'*, and is certainly not a reliable strategy. It is important that the customer has a clear understanding of what the Feature means or does. We can therefore transfer this insight into the next definition: *An Advantage explains what the feature means or does.*

For example:
- *Which gives you unconditional cover for a full five years.*
- *Which means that you're getting excellent value for money.*
- *So that you can download files confidently.*

Benefit

A Benefit Statement appears to be exactly the same as an Advantage Statement. It also explains what a Feature means or does, but with one major difference. A Benefit explains *how a Feature of a product or service will answer a specific need expressed by the customer.*

Yet another mistake made by salespeople is to 'spray' customers with a long list of irrelevant Advantages. How would you feel if you were the customer? You can imagine what's probably going through the customer's mind at that time. This egregious strategy can actually cause Objections to the sale. Now why would anyone want to create objections for themselves?

Preparing Product Profiles

Now let's get back to the question of developing one's product knowledge. The salesperson needs to work out all the Features and Advantages for each of the products and services in the range. Although it seems quite pedantic, it is necessary to point out that you can't prepare Benefit Statements in advance. You don't know exactly what your client's Needs are going to be. You can however, prepare Features and Advantages for each product and service that once learned, can be appropriately used when the client expresses a Need.

Always use the words **YOU** or **YOUR** when preparing an Advantage Statement. This will ensure that you focus on how the product or service helps the customer, rather than just providing a technical explanation. Write out each Feature and Advantage Statement in full, using the exact words you'll be using to communicate with customers and you'll find that the learning process is made much easier. For example: *"This has Velcro straps (Feature) so that you are able to adjust them quickly to a comfortable tension." (Advantage).*

Summary

The life of the professional salesperson is dynamic and skill-based and although the company should provide training, guidance and direction, it is ultimately the sales consultant's responsibility to stay in touch with the constant changes in order to be effective in representing the company to the customer. Using the FAB approach to learn and communicate product knowledge will prove to be quick and effective as well as promote excellent customer service by focusing on the customer's expressed specific needs.

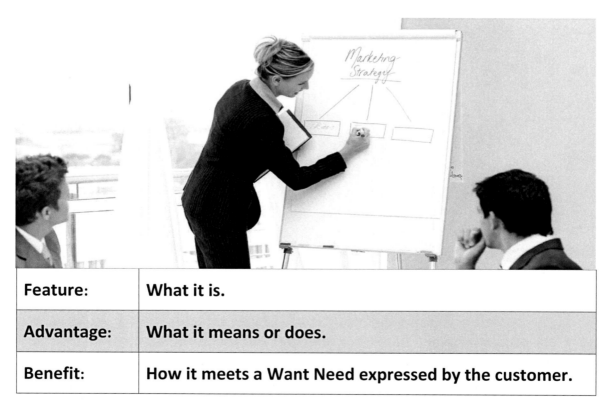

Feature:	What it is.
Advantage:	What it means or does.
Benefit:	How it meets a Want Need expressed by the customer.

Handling Conflict
Avoiding Defend/Attack

A Defend/Attack occurs when discussions become emotionally heated, and value-loaded behaviours are used to attack or make an emotional defence. The result, whether one is defending or attacking, is the same - negative and destructive.

The ego is that part of us that wants to be seen, heard, and valued and so we have a natural desire to be liked; loved; understood; listened to; involved; included; paid attention to, etc. This natural and mostly unconscious intention often drives us to clash with others as we strive to get our point across. Being understood and gaining positive attention is vital to our psychological well-being but it is all eroded when we engage in Defend/Attack behaviour. When someone is 'pushing your button', it is natural to want to push back but when you do, it is often at the expense of a good relationship.

"Try and understand *my* point of view!"

Think back to the last time you were in some kind of disagreement or argument (a Defend/Attack spiral). Regardless of the words you were using, what you were really saying was, *"Listen to me, just understand my point of view, the way I'm feeling, and then you'll understand that my point is valid and we can carry on as normal."* And what was the other person saying at the same time? *"Listen to me, just understand my point of view, the way I'm feeling, and then you'll understand that my point is valid and we can carry on as normal".* Both are struggling to be understood but neither is listening to understand. Listening is the key principle to help avoid conflict and Defend/Attack situations. Both parties are eager to be heard, seen and valued and so it is important that you begin by being the first to understand and only then, to be understood. It doesn't work the other way around.

This is not easy when emotions are high and you want to make yourself understood. Most people listen from their own perspective, in other words from a point of, 'How does this affect *me*?' We need however to understand the other person's point of view and to listen from *their* perspective not ours. How is what they are saying affecting *them*? How are *they* feeling about what they are saying? This is what is meant by 'Listening to Understand'.

Is it more important for you to be right or to be happy?

What is your intention in this kind of interaction? Are you attempting to find a solution or are you trying to lay blame or prove who is right or wrong? This energy of blame always makes a bad situation worse. Being right or defending a position takes a lot of energy and often causes conflict and disconnection.

Defending oneself or attacking someone else is missing the point. It focuses on the person rather than on the issue. A Defend/Attack is always personal and typically provokes a retaliating attack or defence in response. For example, "You never listen to what I am saying." Or, "Hey! I was just trying to help." A Defend/Attack is a 'push style' responding to a 'push style' and the result is that neither party wins. For example, "You were the one who said he would be there!" "Yes, but you were the one who forgot to tell me the meeting was in your office!" A Defend/Attack is always destructive in some way and usually spirals and causes major friction in relationships.

Imagine the following scenario - a husband arrives home and says...

Hi honey, I'm home (or words to that effect).	Simple statement.
Hi sweetheart, did you get the milk?	Simple question.
Did I get the milk?! Give me a break, I've been on the road for two hours after working non-stop for ten hours and all you want to know is.....	Defend/Attack (Try and understand how I am feeling!).
(Interrupting....) *Hey! I just asked if you brought the milk.*	Defending - which has the same impact as attacking - another way of saying "Don't give me a hard time".
Just asked! You're nagging as always.	Defend/Attack.
Nagging? As if you never nag, you're always nagging me about your shirts.	Defend/Attack.
Well why don't you just iron them instead of waiting for me to remind you?	Defend/Attack.
What! Do you think I've got nothing to do but be your slave? What do you ever do for me?	Defend/Attack.
Oh, so who helped your mum with her garden on Saturday?	Defend/Attack.
About bloody time too! The first time in eleven years.	Defend/Attack.
Yes but I did it didn't I? You just can't ever give me credit when I do a good job, you're always...........	And on and on and on......................

Characteristics of a Defend/Attack

There are numerous Defend/Attacks in the above exchange - a spiral. But even just one can be destructive. Here are the main characteristics of this type of interaction:

It's Always Personal

A Defend/Attack is always personal. The intention is to blame, ridicule, deflate, or belittle the other person even if done defensively. It is not a behaviour that will build, maintain, or nurture a relationship. And after all that heated discussion, where's the milk? Did you notice that neither of the people above focused on the issue at hand, the milk. So where did all the frustration come from? Possibly by them not having expressed issues appropriately at the time. The quicker an issue or behaviour is addressed, the easier it is to have the conversation.

It is Always Destructive

Who wins this type of argument? You might think you do, for example, *"No-one talks to me like that!"* (Yes they do but you don't know how to handle it). Or, *"Ha, I really told her!"* (Yes, but now she's leaving you!). Regardless of the situation, a Defend/Attack is always destructive and often spirals out of control. Even in humour or what we often refer to as banter or 'Taking the Mickey', a Defend /Attack can hurt on some level (remember the phrase 'Many a true word said in jest?').

Push - Push

A Defend/Attack is a push style responding to a push style which is one of the causes of conflict. **"Yes but"** is a typical example of this type of response. You can't have a Defend/Attack spiral if one of the parties is using a 'Pull' style. See some of the 'Pull' alternatives below.

Alternatives to a Defend/Attack

> **Apologising doesn't mean that you were wrong or the other person was right. It just means that you value your relationship more than your ego.**

Let it go!

If it's not important, let it go! And sometimes even when it is important, apologising doesn't mean that you were wrong or the other person was right. It just means that you value your relationship more than your ego. Most people argue, confront, and fight over practically anything, turning their lives into a series of battles over relatively insignificant issues. It makes more sense to choose your confrontations wisely and sometimes let others have the satisfaction of being right.

Listen to understand

You can stop the spiral of stubbornness by being the first person to reach out and listen. It's not a competition. Push your emotions aside and listen from *their* perspective not yours. Consider how *they* are feeling and how what they are saying is affecting *them*.

Test your understanding

Ask questions to make sure you understand what the other person is saying before even attempting a response.

Respond with empathy

They want to be understood as much as you do and they aren't ready to understand your point of view until they feel understood. Responding with empathy shows that you *are* trying to understand. You can't however respond with empathy unless you have been listening with empathy. In other words, you need to first listen and try to understand how they are feeling before you can respond appropriately. Simply consider how you think *they* are feeling and check it out. For example, "You seem to be quite *worried* about how long it is taking?" When responding with empathy, remember to relate back both *the* FEELING and the CONTENT. For example, "You seem to be *annoyed* (feeling) *that I didn't get there on time* (content)?" **But don't be sarcastic**. That would be just another form of Defend/Attack.

Wait three seconds

We often react to criticism emotionally and impulsively by saying the first thing that comes to mind. Waiting a few seconds after the person finishes talking will give you time to consider your reaction. It will also:

- Allow them to finish speaking.
- Give you time to try and understand what is being said.
- Give you time to consider what you really want from the transaction.
- Prevent you from reacting impulsively and emotionally.
- Help you cope with difficult situations especially when you need time to think of an appropriate and constructive response.

Remember however that too intense a silence will be uncomfortable and achieve the opposite effect.

Focus on the issue not the person

Keep your focus on the topic at hand. Ask questions about the issue and seek or propose a solution.

Use a Feelings Commentary

"I'm feeling a bit concerned that this seems like an argument. I certainly don't want to argue with you, how can I help fix this?"

A Feelings Commentary is an extremely effective way of building trust, strengthening relationships and communicating openly and assertively. It is also known as 'responsibility language'. Instead of attacking someone by saying something like, *"You make me angry,"* take ownership of the communication by saying how you are feeling, for example, *"I feel quite disappointed that you forgot to bring the tickets after I reminded you about them."*

A Feelings Commentary shows your openness and willingness to talk constructively about an issue, which usually encourages openness and trust from the other person. For example, *"I'm feeling quite uncomfortable about what happened at our last meeting."* Or, *"I'm a bit worried about how to proceed from this point, and I would welcome any suggestions you might have."*

Nurture Relationships

Everyone has an inherent need to feel heard, seen, and valued. Avoid getting hooked into *any* Defend/Attack situation. Enhance or at least maintain the self-esteem of others at all times and you can be assured of much improved relationships.

"Too often we underestimate the power of a touch, a smile, a kind word, a listening ear, an honest compliment, or the smallest act of caring, all of which have the potential to turn a life around." *Leo Buscaglia*

Presenting With Impact!

The Nature of Presentations

The nature of presentations has changed considerably. The novelty of slick PowerPoint slides is no longer enough to attract and hold attention and certainly not enough to persuade people to take action towards a pre-determined objective. Even the typical environment has changed. Presentations now also take place across desks, tables, in restaurants, hotel reception areas, etc. Engagement is the key. Presentations are essentially about engagement and influencing an audience towards a pre-planned objective. Here are some essential tips to help you deliver all kinds of presentations with impact.

Tips and Techniques

Objective

Your intention for the presentation will drive everything else - the planning, content, impact, etc. Ask yourself, *"Why am I giving this particular presentation?"* *"What is it that I am hoping to achieve at the end of it?"* *"What action do I want the audience to take?"* *"How will I know when I've been successful?"* Without a clear-cut objective it is very difficult to plan your strategy and structure. The following will provide the basic guidelines for an effective structure.

The Introduction (tell them what you are going to tell them)

Gain the full attention of your audience from the very beginning. Your introduction should contain an attention-grabber, an agenda, a clarification of the audience's requirements, and agreement to the proposed structure.

The Body (tell them)

Once you have clearly defined your presentation objective, it's time to identify the issues that will enable you to put your message across. Each of your main points must link up in such a way that the audience will understand how it impacts upon their requirements. Each point must also be able to stand on its own with its own benefit statements, visual aids and other supporting data, to allow you to flex your presentation to your audience's needs on the day.

Once you have planned your main points, the next step is to prioritise them. Take note of the points at the bottom of your list. It might be better to leave them out completely than risk diluting the more powerful statements.

The Summary (tell them what you have told them)

Although it may seem redundant to repeat the major points and benefits, don't fail to do so. Repetition aids retention and provides clarity. Be careful not to fade out. Just as you created impact with your introduction, you must also end with a powerful conclusion.

Gaining Commitment (ask them what they think about it)

Unless your presentation is purely an information-giving session, there is almost always something that you want your audience to *do* as a result of your presentation. For example:

- To buy your idea.
- To accept your strategy.
- To implement your strategy.
- To approve your budget.
- To support your venture.

Visual Aids

The proper use of visual aids is to achieve something in your presentation that cannot be achieved effectively using words alone. In other words, visuals must support your presentation and not be used to make your point for you. It is the combined impact of the visual and vocal that gets the message across effectively. Don't place the major emphasis on visual aids and relegate yourself to the minor role of narrator.

- You should always be in control. The visual is an *aid* and must never become more important than the presenter.

- Use presentation media appropriately and responsibly. Don't use slides out of habit. Most people have heard the phrase, 'Death by PowerPoint' so don't use slides if they are not appropriate. Avoid using a slide presentation to small groups of people unless absolutely necessary and avoid using Flipcharts when talking to large groups of people.

- Become thoroughly familiar with operating the equipment beforehand.

- Ensure that your visuals are large enough for everyone to read and simple enough for everyone to understand.

- Avoid reading word-for-word. The audience will be reading faster than you will be speaking, and will not be listening. Allow the audience enough time to read and take in the images and then remove them as soon as you move on to the next point.

- Stop talking whenever you glance at your notes, visuals, etc. Maintain eye-contact whenever speaking.

Voice Techniques and Gravitas

Most people have a relatively short attention span. People think at a rate of four to seven times faster than they talk. This means that if you don't arrest their attention, they will probably end up day-dreaming. It's your responsibility to keep the audience engaged at all times by relating what you are saying to their specific needs and situation. You also need to express confidence, show enthusiasm, and demonstrate a lively interest in what you are saying. Give of yourself; use examples and stories from your personal and professional life to elaborate and bring your message to life. To monitor your impact, ask yourself:

- Am I bored?
- Am I speaking automatically or being mechanical?
- Am I reciting word-for-word?
- Am I making sense?
- Am I addressing their needs?
- Am I in teacher mode?
- Am I projecting enjoyment of the presentation?
- Is my voice crisp and clear?

In order for the audience to understand your message, they need to hear what you have to say. Always face your audience, project your voice and speak clearly. Open your mouth and purposely form your words.

To hold the attention of your audience, project with gravitas and punctuate your delivery by varying the **TONE** of your voice; the **PITCH** of your voice; the **LOUDNESS** of your delivery; and the **RATE** of your speech.

Gravitas - Calm; Professional; Respectful; Dignified; Assertive; Impact!

Gravitas is a quality of substance or depth of personality. It's presenting dignity, a serious or dignified demeanour. To develop and project Gravitas:

- Face the audience with confidence and maintain eye contact.
- Make an impact even before you start to speak by considering what you are about to say before saying it. Start with a few seconds of eye-contact and then once you've made the connection, begin to speak calmly. Talk at a steady, measured pace.
- Speak consciously. Eliminate all the unnecessary 'Fillers' from your speech such as, 'Uhm', 'ah', 'You know', and any other unnecessary irritators.
- Avoid unnecessary 'Softeners'. There are times when it is important to 'soften' your message in order to be sensitive towards a particular situation. However, there are many times when it is unsuitable and undermines your assertiveness and credibility. Beware of words such as, 'Sort of' 'Kind of' 'Perhaps' 'Probably' 'Possibly' and 'I think' (when you are certain).
- Pause for a few seconds to allow significant points to sink in. Ensure you maintain eye-contact whilst doing so. Get comfortable with silence.
- Give your undivided attention when others are speaking and when they have finished, don't rush to answer. Wait a few seconds and consider what they have said before responding.
- Ensure that your talk is structured, logical and easy to follow. Keep your message and content concise, clear, and to the point.

Dealing With Anxiety and Nerves

Mark Twain said, "There are two types of speakers: those who are nervous and those who are liars." Everyone has some anxiety when speaking in front of a group of people. The way to deal with this anxiety is to acknowledge that the fear is perfectly normal and then ensure you prepare thoroughly. Here are some top tips that will get you to the level required not only to deliver a successful presentation but also to enable you to enjoy presenting.

- Check the facilities and equipment in advance. Ensure that your audience will be comfortable and well-positioned to see all visuals.
- Obtain information about the audience beforehand. Learn their names and use them.
- Know your objective, subject, material and be able to operate the presentation equipment.
- Prepare a carefully structured outline; set up prompts, and practise.
- Consider which methods of participation you will be able to use. In order to obtain commitment, understanding, retention and rapport, you need to *involve* your audience.
- Anticipate problems and prepare ways to cope with them. Practise responses to tough questions or objections.
- Identify your fears. Confront them and transform them into realistic affirmations.
- Introduce yourself in advance. Arrive early and chat.
- Manage your appearance. Dress comfortably and appropriately.
- Assume that the audience is on your side. Act *as if* you are confident.
- Do not rush to speak. Wait until the audience is settled and then provide an overview and objective of the presentation.
- Give special emphasis to the first five minutes. Rehearse this and deliver it without notes.
- Ensure that you understand the needs of your audience and *keep your focus on them at all times*. Talk *to, and with* your audience, not at them. Be natural and use your own style and words, speak from your beliefs and convictions.
- Maintain eye-contact at all times and listen! Listen with the intention to understand.

Handling Questions and Objections

By anticipating questions and objections before your presentation, you can prepare strategies and adjust the content so as to avoid uncomfortable situations. If they do arise, the following steps will help you to cope with them professionally and effectively:

Handling Questions

1. Listen with the intention of understanding.
2. Check your understanding.
3. Answer clearly and concisely.

Handling Objections

1. Listen with the intention of understanding.
2. Check your understanding.
3. Ask a need-seeking question.
4. Answer with a Benefit statement.

Coaching Self-Assessment

If you would like a *free* printable copy of this document, please request it via email (contact details on the last page of this book).

Self-Assessment

How do you currently feel about your life? Complete the following for *each* area on the next pages:

Satisfaction

Rate your level of satisfaction by circling a number from 1 (most dissatisfied) to 10 (most satisfied).

Personal strengths

List your strengths in these areas. These can include anything from having a healthy level of physical fitness, being committed to getting into shape, or adhering to a detailed budget plan, etc.

Achievements

List your achievements. Ask yourself what you are proud of; what you have accomplished that has brought meaning to your life; what positive qualities and skills you possess; what you have done that makes you happy; has made others happy; has made a positive impact on your life and on others.

Immediate challenges / blocks / problems

List any negative issues or problems that affect you. Make sure you focus upon yourself, for example, *"I struggle to communicate when I am anxious."*

Specific actions

List one specific action that YOU could take that would result in you being able to give yourself a higher satisfaction rating. Ensure that the action is specific, in other words, it describes:

- What you will actually be doing.
- How you will be doing it.
- How *well* you will be doing it.
- When you will be doing it.
- When you will have completed it.
- How you will know when you have been successful.
- What support you might need from others in order to achieve it.

Family / Extended Family	Dissatisfied ⟶ Satisfied									
	1	2	3	4	5	6	7	8	9	10
Personal Strengths:										
Achievements:										
Immediate challenges / blocks / problems:										
Specific actions:										

Finance	Dissatisfied ⟶ Satisfied									
	1	2	3	4	5	6	7	8	9	10
Personal Strengths:										
Achievements:										
Immediate challenges / blocks / problems:										
Specific actions:										

Friends / Social Life	Dissatisfied ⟶ Satisfied									
	1	2	3	4	5	6	7	8	9	10
Personal Strengths:										
Achievements:										
Immediate challenges / blocks / problems:										
Specific actions:										

Health	Dissatisfied									Satisfied
	1	2	3	4	5	6	7	8	9	10
Personal Strengths:										
Achievements:										
Immediate challenges / blocks / problems:										
Specific actions:										

Hobbies / Sports	Dissatisfied									Satisfied
	1	2	3	4	5	6	7	8	9	10
Personal Strengths:										
Achievements:										
Immediate challenges / blocks / problems:										
Specific actions:										

Personal Relationships	Dissatisfied									Satisfied
	1	2	3	4	5	6	7	8	9	10
Personal Strengths:										
Achievements:										
Immediate challenges / blocks / problems:										
Specific actions:										

Physical Home Environment	Dissatisfied ⟶ Satisfied									
	1	2	3	4	5	6	7	8	9	10
Personal Strengths:										
Achievements:										
Immediate challenges / blocks / problems:										
Specific actions:										

Self-Development / Growth	Dissatisfied ⟶ Satisfied									
	1	2	3	4	5	6	7	8	9	10
Personal Strengths:										
Achievements:										
Immediate challenges / blocks / problems:										
Specific actions:										

Spiritual / Religious Life	Dissatisfied ⟶ Satisfied									
	1	2	3	4	5	6	7	8	9	10
Personal Strengths:										
Achievements:										
Immediate challenges / blocks / problems:										
Specific actions:										

Work Relationships	Dissatisfied									Satisfied
	1	2	3	4	5	6	7	8	9	10
Personal Strengths:										
Achievements:										
Immediate challenges / blocks / problems:										
Specific actions:										

Work / Career Overall	Dissatisfied									Satisfied
	1	2	3	4	5	6	7	8	9	10
Personal Strengths:										
Achievements:										
Immediate challenges / blocks / problems:										
Specific actions:										

Other	Dissatisfied									Satisfied
	1	2	3	4	5	6	7	8	9	10
Personal Strengths:										
Achievements:										
Immediate challenges / blocks / problems:										
Specific actions:										

Overall Satisfaction Grid

Without referring back to any of your ratings, complete the following overall satisfaction grid. Rate your satisfaction by circling a number for each of the areas listed below and add any other significant areas in your life to 'Other'.

	Dissatisfied									Satisfied
Family / extended family:	1	2	3	4	5	6	7	8	9	10
Finance:	1	2	3	4	5	6	7	8	9	10
Friends / social life:	1	2	3	4	5	6	7	8	9	10
Health:	1	2	3	4	5	6	7	8	9	10
Hobbies / sports:	1	2	3	4	5	6	7	8	9	10
Personal relationships:	1	2	3	4	5	6	7	8	9	10
Physical home environment:	1	2	3	4	5	6	7	8	9	10
Self-development / growth:	1	2	3	4	5	6	7	8	9	10
Spiritual / religious life:	1	2	3	4	5	6	7	8	9	10
Work relationships:	1	2	3	4	5	6	7	8	9	10
Work / career - overall:	1	2	3	4	5	6	7	8	9	10
Other:	1	2	3	4	5	6	7	8	9	10

Action Plan

Now it is time to take action. Why not begin by setting a goal for the area you rated lowest? Make sure the goal is written in a way that will crystallise your thoughts and help motivate you to take the action required. List a specific action you could take that would raise your satisfaction level. To ensure that the action is specific, it must describe:

- What you will actually be doing.
- How you will be doing it.
- How well you will be doing it.
- When you will be doing it.
- When you will have completed it.
- How you will know when you have been successful
- What support you might need from others to achieve it.

Make a list, preferably in your diary, of at least one specific action per week required to increase your satisfaction levels. Remember to list dates for each one and prioritise them realistically. These dates or deadlines should be both challenging and realistic.

Stress Buster
Self-Assessment and Action Plan

If you would like a *free* printable copy of this document, please request it via email (contact details on the last page of this book).

Plan your own ideal stress-busting programme. How do you currently rate yourself in the following important factors that impact on how you manage stress? Complete the following for each area on the next pages:

Your Satisfaction Rating
Rate your level of satisfaction by circling a number from 1 (most dissatisfied) to 10 (most satisfied).

Your Personal Strengths
List your strengths in these areas. These can include anything from getting regular exercise, being open about your feelings, using a diary effectively, correcting negative thoughts, etc.

Your Achievements
List your achievements in each area Ask yourself what you are proud of; what you have accomplished that has worked for you; what positive qualities and skills do you possess; what you have done that makes you happy; has made others happy; has made a positive impact on your life and on others.

Immediate challenges / blocks / problems
List any negative issues or problems that affect you. Make sure you focus upon yourself, for example, *"I struggle to communicate when I am anxious."*

Specific Actions You Will Be Taking
List one specific action that **you** could take that would result in you being able to give yourself a higher satisfaction rating. Ensure that the action is specific, in other words, it describes:

- What you will actually be doing.
- How you will be doing it.
- How *well* you will be doing it.
- When you will be doing it.
- When you will have completed it.
- How you will know when you have been successful
- What support you might need from others in order to achieve it.

Relaxation methods	Dissatisfied ⟶ Satisfied									
	1	2	3	4	5	6	7	8	9	10
What am I good at?										
Achievements										
Immediate challenges / blocks / problems										
Specific actions *Find a method that suits you*										

Exercise	Dissatisfied ⟶ Satisfied									
	1	2	3	4	5	6	7	8	9	10
What am I good at?										
Achievements										
Immediate challenges / blocks / problems										
Specific actions *Burn up the bio-chemicals and restore the balance*										

Sleep	Dissatisfied ⟶ Satisfied									
	1	2	3	4	5	6	7	8	9	10
What am I good at?										
Achievements										
Immediate challenges / blocks / problems										
Specific actions *Improve patterns and adopt a routine*										

Time Management	Dissatisfied ———————————————→ Satisfied									
	1	2	3	4	5	6	7	8	9	10
What am I good at?										
Achievements										
Immediate challenges / blocks / problems										
Specific actions *Prioritise and delegate*										

Communication Skills	Dissatisfied ———————————————→ Satisfied									
	1	2	3	4	5	6	7	8	9	10
What am I good at?										
Achievements										
Immediate challenges / blocks / problems										
Specific actions *Share problems and listen to others*										

Positive Thinking	Dissatisfied ———————————————→ Satisfied									
	1	2	3	4	5	6	7	8	9	10
What am I good at?										
Achievements										
Immediate challenges / blocks / problems										
Specific actions *Counter negative thinking with positive thoughts and affirmations*										

Healthy Nutrition	Dissatisfied → Satisfied									
	1	2	3	4	5	6	7	8	9	10
What am I good at?										
Achievements										
Immediate challenges / blocks / problems										
Specific actions *Avoid excessive use of alcohol, caffeine, nicotine and sugars*										

Assertiveness	Dissatisfied → Satisfied									
	1	2	3	4	5	6	7	8	9	10
What am I good at?										
Achievements										
Immediate challenges / blocks / problems										
Specific actions *Take action to modify aggressive or passive behaviour patterns*										

Socialising	Dissatisfied → Satisfied									
	1	2	3	4	5	6	7	8	9	10
What am I good at?										
Achievements										
Immediate challenges / blocks / problems										
Specific actions *Schedule time for social contact with friends*										

Emotional Needs	Dissatisfied ⟶ Satisfied									
	1	2	3	4	5	6	7	8	9	10
What am I good at?										
Achievements										
Immediate challenges / blocks / problems										
Specific actions *Laughter; crying; sharing thoughts or worries with a confidant helps*										

Avoiding Stressors	Dissatisfied ⟶ Satisfied									
	1	2	3	4	5	6	7	8	9	10
What am I good at?										
Achievements										
Immediate challenges / blocks / problems										
Specific actions *Plan to reduce, avoid, or eliminate the things that cause you stress*										

Leisure	Dissatisfied ⟶ Satisfied									
	1	2	3	4	5	6	7	8	9	10
What am I good at?										
Achievements										
Immediate challenges / blocks / problems										
Specific actions *Schedule hobbies, holidays, time with special friends and family*										

Overall Satisfaction Grid

Without referring back to any of your ratings, complete the following overall satisfaction grid. Rate your satisfaction by circling a number for each of the areas listed below.

	Dissatisfied									Satisfied
Relaxation Methods:	1	2	3	4	5	6	7	8	9	10
Exercise:	1	2	3	4	5	6	7	8	9	10
Sleep:	1	2	3	4	5	6	7	8	9	10
Time Management:	1	2	3	4	5	6	7	8	9	10
Communication:	1	2	3	4	5	6	7	8	9	10
Positive Thinking:	1	2	3	4	5	6	7	8	9	10
Good Nutrition:	1	2	3	4	5	6	7	8	9	10
Assertiveness:	1	2	3	4	5	6	7	8	9	10
Socialising:	1	2	3	4	5	6	7	8	9	10
Emotional Needs:	1	2	3	4	5	6	7	8	9	10
Avoiding Stressors:	1	2	3	4	5	6	7	8	9	10
Leisure:	1	2	3	4	5	6	7	8	9	10

Action Plan

Now it is time to take action. Why not begin by setting a goal for the area you rated lowest? Make sure the goal is written in a way that will crystallise your thoughts and help motivate you to take the action required. List a specific action you could take that would raise your satisfaction level. To ensure that the action is specific, it must describe:

- What you will actually be doing.
- How you will be doing it.
- How well you will be doing it.
- When you will be doing it.
- When you will have completed it.
- How you will know when you have been successful
- What support you might need from others to achieve it.

Make a list, preferably in your diary, of at least one specific action per week required to increase your satisfaction levels. Remember to list dates for each one and prioritise them realistically. These dates or deadlines should be both challenging and realistic.

Free Behavioural Needs Analysis

Inspired Behavioural Change

What good is training unless it results in a positive change in individual behaviour? In order to ensure behavioural change, Russ Baleson Training can offer you a free and no obligation, Behavioural Needs Analysis (in the United Kingdom and South Africa).

This will help you assess current behaviour and its specific cause, clarify desired behaviours, and then determine whether training or coaching will provide you with an appropriate solution and a return on your investment.

Customised Training Workshops

Russ Baleson Training will customise programmes specifically for your company. All content is tailored and continuously adjusted to meet both the company's objectives and each delegate's specific personal needs.

Russ Baleson Training

Inspiring Behavioural Change
The People and Management Training Specialists
http://russbalesontraining.co.uk
russbaleson@gmail.com